a whole person in a whole world

by

harvey potthoff

1908 Grand Avenue
Nashville, Tennessee 37203

With thanks to Larry McCargar
for the gift of his friendship

Be his
My special thanks, whose even-balanced soul
Business could not make dull, nor passion wild;
Who saw life steadily, and saw it whole.

A PERSONAL WORD

This book is for you.

It has to do with the joys and sorrows, the discouragements and the hopes, the failures and achievements, the doubts and the beliefs which are involved in being human.

It has to do with our personal lives—what they mean and what they might mean.

It is written in the conviction that Christian faith brings us the deepest truth about life and offers each of us the possibility for a new and more fulfilling quality of life.

It is an invitation to share in an exploration of what Christian faith has to say to us, and of the new life it offers us.

It is intended to provide help in taking some first steps into the Christian life and then some further steps of growth in that life.

Life is a precious gift. But no one lives under ideal circumstances. Problems and possibilities are interwoven in the pattern of life. This book is intended to reflect on life from a Christian perspective, pointing toward the joy and faith and hope and love which characterize what Paul called the "more excellent way."

Harvey Potthoff
Denver, Colorado
A Day In 1972

CONTENTS

PART ONE

OUR HUNGER FOR WHOLENESS

"Things fall apart; the centre cannot hold. . . ."
William Yeats

"And does this empty silence have to be?
And is there no-one there at all
To answer me?"
Eithne Tabor

"Man's development requires his capacity to transcend the narrow prison of his ego, his greed, his selfishness, his separation from his fellow man, and, hence, his basic loneliness."
Erich Fromm

"Do you want to be healed?"
Jesus

BEGINNING WHERE WE ARE

Today is the first day of the rest of your life.
Yesterday has been lived. Tomorrow is still unborn.
But today is now ours. What meaning can today—
yes, this very hour—have for us? Perhaps it could
mark the taking of some first step into a new life.
Perhaps it could mark the taking of some further
step in a new life we have recently entered. In
any event, let not this day—this hour—pass without
meaning.

Let us agree at the outset to try to be honest with
ourselves. Do we really want things to be different
than they are? Do we really want a better life? And
do we want these things enough that we are open
to being changed?

If our answer is "yes" to these questions, we need
to be honest with ourselves at still another point. We
need to be honest in facing up to the realities of our
present situation. A journey of a thousand miles
begins with a single step. We take that first step
from where we are now.

Each person brings so many things to the present
moment. There are influences from out of the past—
we all have our histories. There are memories and
hopes, loves and hates, doubts and beliefs, joys and
sorrows. We bring past successes and failures to this
moment. We bring our friendships and our loves to
this moment—but we also bring loneliness, and
sometimes the memory of friendship and loves
which no longer are ours.

9

This morning each of us woke up in the awareness that "I am I and not someone else." Sometimes we are on good terms with ourselves. Other times we feel like Dwight Moody when he said, "I have had more trouble with myself than with any other person I have ever met." We all understand that. We are problems to ourselves. Yet, the gift of life brings with it the call to make something out of ourselves —to be who we are with integrity. Every living person is handicapped and limited in some way. But every living person also is a unique center of experience and center of influence. We are both bound and free. There is possibility in every person's situation.

Beginning where we are means beginning with our own unique makeup and circumstances. We don't have to do any pretending if we are serious about looking for a new life. We are who and what we are. Our human relationships are what they are. The external circumstances of our lives are what they are. That is the starting point. We are told that Peter once asked Jesus about the duties of one of the other disciples. We are told that in that particular situation Jesus said, ". . . what is that to thee? follow *thou* me." The call to the new life of Christian discipleship always comes to us personally, in concrete terms, *where we are*. Christian experience begins with the honest recognition that our lives leave much to be desired, but by the grace of God they can be something better.

In the fourteenth century there lived a man by the name of Meister Eckhart. He was the founder of a religious movement known as the Friends of God. He understood many things about the human spirit and about God's ways in the souls of men. He insisted that no two people follow exactly the same path in their religious pilgrimages. He urged persons to let God into *their* lives—beginning where they were, in their uniqueness. He wrote, "God does not work in all hearts alike. . . . Cherish in yourself the birth of God." Calling each person to the realization of the worth and dignity of his own life, Eckhart wrote:

> That I am a man,
> this I share with other men.
>
> That I see and hear and
> that I eat and drink
> is what all animals do likewise.
>
> But that I am I is only mine
> and belongs to me
> and to nobody else;
> to no other man
> not to an angel nor to God—
> except inasmuch as I am one with Him.

The Christian pilgrimage begins with an honest recognition of who and what and where we are.

Beginning where we are also involves being honest in facing the facts of our world as they are.

There is so much to cause wonder, excitement, gratitude, hope in today's world. But there is also so much of sorrow and of tragedy. Over half of the people on planet earth do not have enough to eat. Thousands die daily from malnutrition and related diseases. The tragedy of war—the killing by man of his fellowmen—is a terrible fact. Multitudes suffer from political persecution and from prejudice in the hearts of their fellowmen. The plundering of our planet, the waste of physical and human resources, the pollution of air and soil and water, the exploitation of life's basic support systems, all endanger the life of man on this planet. In such a world Nicholas Berdyaev asked, ". . . is that being to whom the future belongs to be called man?"

The search for a meaningful life is not simply a private, individual matter. It involves the whole human creation. We need the vision of whole persons in a whole world. Better individuals help to create a better world. But it is also true that a world which is good for living helps persons to be better individuals. The New Testament reminds us that we are members one of another. Indeed, our lives are linked with all creation.

Beginning where we are, let us give thanks for new discoveries being made, for suffering which is be'ng relieved, for new visions of brotherhood, for new efforts at communication among the peoples of the earth. There is so much for which to be grateful and in which we may find hope.

But let us also be realistic in recognizing that our individual destinies are interrelated with those of others—and with the natural world. God's world is a *whole* world. The parts are related. God calls us to aspire after wholeness—in our personal lives, in our relationships, in our world.

On the outskirts of a small town there is a sign which reads, "This is a good town for living." We seek communities which support and nurture good living. We seek institutions which support and nurture good living. We seek a world which is good for human living. Whole persons in a whole world—that is our goal—beginning where we are!

THE COURAGE TO GO BEYOND WHERE WE ARE

Deep within nature there seems to be an urge to grow and to achieve fulfillment.

Placed in suitable surroundings the seed germinates, swells, sends out roots, sends up a sprout, and ultimately produces seed after its kind.

Loren Eisley writes, "I have seen a tree root burst a rock face on a mountain or slowly wrench aside the gateway of a forgotten city. . . . A kind of desperate will resides even in a root."

A young bird displays an inner compulsion to learn to fly, to leave the nest, to sing, to mate, to care for its young, to migrate.

So it is with human beings. There seems to be an inner urge or propulsion to move through various stages, moving toward fulfillment of life, toward wholeness.

Psychologists have used various terms in speaking of a person's deep-rooted urge to go beyond where he is and to find fulfillment. Gordon Allport says that man is a creature whose nature calls for "becoming" something new. He writes, "Happiness is the glow that attends the integration of the person while pursuing or contemplating the attainment of goals." Abraham Maslow said that man is often moved by "growth motives." Deep within, human beings seek "self-actualization." Carl Rogers insists that the basic motive of the human organism is to actualize, maintain, and enhance itself.

There are those who believe that the urge for growth and fulfillment is basic in the natural world. Harlow Shapley, the astronomer, has written of "the greatest operation of nature—an operation of cosmic dimensions that might simply be called Growth." Perhaps one recalls the lines of Lowell:

Every clod feels a stir of might,
An instinct within it that reaches and towers
And, groping blindly above it for light,
Climbs to a soul in grass and flowers.

Insofar as human beings share in creation it is reasonable to suppose that they, too, cannot rest content with things as they are. There is an urge to go on, to explore, to move into new worlds of experience, to grow. When man loses the spirit of adventure he begins to die.

Christian faith insists that more than man's own nature is involved in the urge to grow and find fulfillment. God is in it. Christians find in Jesus Christ their supreme clue to what life is all about—to what God is doing in the world. And as the New Testament makes clear, the call of Jesus Christ is a call to moving beyond where one is, into new lands of experience and service. The letter to the Ephesians puts it this way: ". . . until we all attain to the unity of the faith and of the knowledge of the Son of God, to mature manhood, to the measure of the stature of the fullness of Christ; . . . speaking the truth in love, we are to grow up in every way into him who is the head, into Christ." (Ephesians 4:13-15)

We are called to go beyond where we are. That message comes to us from the world of nature, from the depths of our own natures, from the God declared in Jesus Christ. In the divine order of things we are permitted and encouraged to push on and to hope. But beneath the surface of our lives a tug of war goes on. There is the urge to progress—but there is also an urge to regress. There is the urge to push ahead; but there is also the urge to shrink back. Life is hard and threatening. Sometimes the urge is strong to seek a safe retreat—a return to the womb. We recall the Old Testament story of Lot's wife, looking backward and unable to go forward, immobilized into a pillar of salt! So, there are those who seem unable to escape from the desolation of their own spirits.

But the biblical story is a story of the God who says, "Behold, I make all things new," and who keeps calling persons to go beyond where they are, into new lands of habitation and experience. The God of biblical faith moves in history and calls persons to move with him. *Biblical faith involves the courage to go beyond where we are—with God's help.*

Abraham was in a comfortable enough situation, but the call came to make a journey in which there was no turning back "to the land that I will show you." (Genesis 12:1)

The death of King Uzziah seemed to some to shake the very foundations of life. In this time of discouragement the young Isaiah went into the temple. There the awesome and wondrous sense of God's presence came to him. In this setting he heard the words: "Whom shall I send and who will go for us?" In the depths of his being Isaiah found himself responding, "Here I am! Send me." (Isaiah 6:1-8)

Uprooted from their homeland, deported to the foreign land of Babylon, some dispirited Hebrews asked "How can we sing the Lord's song in a strange land?" To them there came the voice of the prophet

15

calling them to go beyond their limited concepts of God to a greater understanding of *the God who is in all lands and who will strengthen and empower them in their new situation.* (Isaiah 40:27-31)

Saul endeavored to live within the perspectives of his inherited faith. But deep within a desperate battle was going on. In the agony of the struggle he lashed out in hostility. Under these circumstances there came to him a light and call to go beyond his present state. We know the revolutionary results of that! (Acts 9)

So we might go on, recalling persons who learned that at the heart of life and in the depths of reality there is a summons to go beyond where we are. Life is not intended to stand still. There is movement, direction, purpose in it.

This would indeed be a wondrous day or hour for each of us if we could come to know that things need not remain just as they are. Indeed, things **cannot** remain just as they are. In an external sense little may seem to be changed sometimes. But there can be profound changes in what life means to us in how we experience life.

E. E. Cummings wrote, "We can never be born enough. . . . Miracles are to come. With you I leave a remembrance of miracles; they are by somebody who can love and who shall be continually reborn. . . ." Is it too good to be true that you can really go beyond where you are? That you can find a life of deeper meaning and fulfillment than you have known?

Christian faith affirms the reality of a new being, a new creation, a new life in the spirit. Paul, who knew a great deal from personal experience about these matters, wrote to the Corinthians, ". . . if anyone is in Christ, he is a new creation; the old has passed away, behold, the new has come." (2 Corinthians 5:17)

Many persons who had supposed they were up against a blank wall, or that they had reached the end of their rope, or that for them life could be nothing more than a weary routine, have discovered that Paul was right. There is such a thing as the courage to go beyond where we are. There is a new life in the spirit. God moves in the hearts and relationships of persons—sometimes when they least expect it!

SEEING LIFE IN A DIFFERENT WAY

Persons are likely to continue in their usual styles of life unless they come to a new outlook on life. Significant changes take place only when one comes to see life in a different way. We tend to be formed in the light of our basic images of self and others and life.

Some years ago I visited a rock shop in a small town in the state of Wyoming. The shop was in an old building which once housed a gambling establishment. The rocks were on old gambling tables. I noticed a door in one corner over which there was a sign which read "The Crying Room." I asked the elderly proprietor what that was all about. "That is where the gamblers could go and express their feelings in private after losing at the tables," he said. "Come in and see what we have in there now," he went on. We entered the very small room. On shelves were some ordinary looking rocks. If I had seen them on a hillside, I would have walked on. Apparently the proprietor sensed my skepticism. He closed the door. The room was in total darkness. He then turned an ultraviolet light on the rocks, and immediately there came forth colors of indescribable beauty.

For me that was no crying room. It was a place where a deep truth became clearer. *It makes all the difference in the world in what light we see life.*

So often we see just the surface of life. Things appear to be so ordinary, so commonplace. But sometimes we are enabled to see deeper. Then it is that we begin to discover possibilities and meanings we had missed before.

The Christian gospel is light on life. In this light we come to know that life is not just on the surface. We come to know of a depth and wonder and possibility we may have missed before. Ordinary persons and ordinary events and ordinary experiences seem less ordinary. There is a sanctity in existence. In this light our problems take on a new kind of significance. In this light all creation comes alive in a new way. We see, and feel, and experience the world in a new way. In this light something within us dies, and something new is born. In this light it is given us to know that indeed we *can* go on from where we are!

The Christian gospel assures us that we do not walk alone. Some of our greatest discouragements come when we are fatigued and when we are lonely. Fatigue and loneliness are real—but Christian faith assures us we are not alone in the struggles and aspirations of life. "The Lord is the everlasting God, the Creator of the ends of the earth. . . . He gives power to the faint . . . they who wait for the Lord shall renew their strength." (Isaiah 40:28, 29, 31) "For I am sure that neither death, nor life . . . nor anything else in all creation, will be able to separate us from the love of God in Christ Jesus our Lord." (Romans 8:38-39)

Christian faith assures us that life finds its deepest meanings through relationships—with the good earth, with other persons, with significant causes, and most profoundly, with God. In the fourth century Augustine put it in words the world has never forgotten: "Thou hast made us for thyself, and restless is our heart until it comes to rest in thee." The search for God is our ultimate and most enduring search. The finding of God and being found of God is life's ultimate good. In the light of this faith we all see things in a different way.

Is it not interesting how we sometimes express ways of seeing life in just a word or phrase? We say "Life is just a rat race," or "Life is just a treadmill," or "Life is just one thing after another." What we sometimes fail to see is that in such statements we are saying something about ourselves: rats in a rat race, cogs in a machine, things in a world of things. Is this who and what we really are? Are these images of life and self giving us the deepest truth by which to live?

In our time we are under considerable pressure to adopt still another image of self and of life—that of consumer in a vast production system. Obviously we are all consumers, but when any person adopts a philosophy which says that man is basically a consumer and the best life is a consuming life, he is in deep trouble. Yet, how many advertisers would have us believe that we will truly find the good life if we will just buy and consume their products!

It is encouraging to know that more and more persons are questioning the adequacy of the images of self and life we have just been considering. Many persons are searching for life styles which express other ways of seeing life and other value systems. Among the peoples of the earth there is a hunger for a more fulfilling way of life. It is a hunger for wholeness.

Who can doubt that there is a hunger of the spirit abroad in the world today? It is expressed among persons of all ages. It is as though through some deep promptings of the spirit, more and more people are saying: "It is time that we really probed more deeply into what life is all about."

It is in this time of questioning and searching that we do well to consider two images which emerge out of the Judaic-Christian tradition—*man as a co-creating, celebrating steward, and life as pilgrimage.* These images stand in sharp contrast to those which affirm that basically man is a rat in a rat race, a cog in a machine, a consumer in a system designed primarily for producing things. In the light of these biblical images of steward and pilgrimage we see ourselves and all life in a different way. Like the ultraviolet light, they reveal depths of meaning and possibility we often miss in our living. They challenge us to look deeply into our lives, to reexamine our priorities, to reassess our values. They invite us to go beyond where we are into a more humanly fulfilling quality of life.

To be a co-creating, celebrating steward is to find joy in accepting the gift of life. More than a cog or a thing, man is entrusted with the responsible use of God's creation. The natural world is ours to inhabit, to employ, and to enjoy, but not to exploit or plunder. As stewards we are invited to share in the creating work of God—helping to create relationships and institutions and communities and environments which nurture human growth and dignity. As stewards we are given our times and places in history, called to relate to the needs and demands of the moments of life which are ours. To live our days in the sense of stewardship is to live in the joy and dignity of those who truly bear the image of God.

To see life as pilgrimage is to understand that life has direction, purpose, cumulative meaning. The

21

cycles and seasons of life constitute a pattern, in harmony with which life can grow in fullness of spirit. Life is meant to unfold through the experiences and crises and opportunities which the various chapters of life bring. Persons are born for becoming greater in heart and mind and spirit.

The most important question at journey's end is not how fast did we travel, how many places did we go, how many things did we accumulate, how much power did we exercise over others, but what meanings did life come to hold? What kind of persons did we become? Did we contribute to human well-being? Did we invest in significant causes which outlast us? Did we grow in oneness with God?

In one of his poems Robert Browning portrays an aged man looking back over his life. He finds deep satisfaction in high endeavors, even though he did not always reach his goals. He finds satisfaction in the struggles of the soul through which he grew in strength and integrity. He finds satisfaction in the memory of true love and friendship and service. He finds satisfaction in outliving problems he once thought were insurmountable. In the memory and sense of fulfillment through all of this the aged man looks ahead to more of pilgrimage in trust and in expectancy, saying, "The Future I may face, now I have proved the Past." Would that each of us might achieve such a high vision of life's meaning! Would that we might see ourselves as stewards of the living God, in pilgrimage throughout the years of our lives. With such a vision we are ready to go further in our quest for a quality of life which fulfills the deeper purposes of God for man.

PART TWO

THERE IS GOOD NEWS TODAY

"From ghoulies and ghosties and long-leggetty beasties
And things that go bump in the night,
Good Lord, deliver us."
(An old Cornish prayer)

"We have fallen upon evil times and the world has waxed very old and wicked. . . . Politics are very corrupt. Children are no longer respectful to their parents."
(From a tablet in the Museum of Constantinople, dated hundreds of years before Christ)

"I am not ashamed of the gospel: it is the power of God for salvation to everyone who has faith. . . ."
(Romans 1:16)

"Brothers, we want you to speak to the people if you have a message of encouragement for them."
(Acts 13:15)

GOOD NEWS ABOUT GOD—
A DEPTH YOU MAY HAVE MISSED

Helen Keller once said that if a person has faith and friends he can stand anything.

Most of us know from experience how precious friendship is. To have someone who knows us and who cares about us is to be truly blessed. Norman Cousins wrote, "All man's history is an endeavor to shatter his loneliness." To have a true friend is to have at least some of the pain of loneliness shattered.

But Helen Keller said one other thing is needed— faith. Are we cared about on an even deeper level than that of human caring? To that crucially important question Christian faith says "Yes."

In the long run, belief in the presence, the power, and the goodness of God tips the scales between despairing and hoping. That is why the Christian gospel is truly good news—it affirms that life is of God, and the God declared in Jesus Christ transforms despair to hope. God's ultimate word to man is not a word of condemnation and despair, but a word of grace and hope.

In every generation there are pessimists who see no grounds for hope. In *The City of Dreadful Night* James Thomson wrote:

"Speak not of comfort where no comfort is
Speak not at all: can words make foul things fair?
Our life's a cheat, our death, a black abyss
Hush and be mute envisaging despair."

That would indeed be a depressing point of view with which to begin a new day, let alone with which to face the harder demands of life.

But all around us are persons who show us that we need not stop on a level of pessimism about life and its prospects. One does not need to close his eyes to the evidence, nor need he surrender his intelligence to believe in God. To be sure, there are some very childish and immature ideas *about* God we need to outgrow. To grow is to outgrow. Strong faith involves outgrowing some of our more limited religious concepts. More positively, there is so much to support trust in a living God.

Leo Tolstoy told of his personal search for a living faith. He experienced doubt and depression. He listened to the testimony of others without avail. At times it seemed to him that there was no way out of the skepticism which was his. Finally, he decided that he would look into the depths of his own life. Instead of listening to the arguments of others, he would examine the testimony of his own experience. It was out of this decision that he wrote, "I remembered that I had lived only when I believed in a God. . . . I only really live when I feel and seek Him." At last he came to say, "Live to seek God, and life will not be without Him."

How does faith in the living God come to be? It varies from person to person. Sometimes it is through the influence of a trusted parent, teacher, friend. Sometimes it is through the teachings of family and church. Scripture and tradition speak their words of witness. But there are those, like Tolstoy, who find the most persuasive testimony to the reality of God *in their own experience*. Faith is kindled when in our own experience we come to the

conviction that every day and every hour we are en-
countering a More-Than-Human REAL OTHER, by
whom we are called to account, but by whom we
are also sustained and brought to newness of life.
No person is an island unto himself. Life springs
from a source deeper than any human source; life
is sustained by a goodness deeper than any human
goodness; life is brought to its fulfillment through a
wisdom and grace greater than any human wisdom
or grace.

Whence comes the deep inner conviction that in life
and in death we are dealing with God? Sometimes
it comes in the awareness that human beings are
not self-sufficient; our arrival and survival depend
on resources greater than our own. Sometimes it
comes in the experience of being judged or called
to account; there are some things we cannot get
away with; there is a built-in judgment in the structures and processes of life. Sometimes it comes
through the experience of a grace and a good beyond our own planning or predicting or producing:
in the experience of healing, deliverance from some
great distress, in the resolution of deep inner conflict, in growth of spirit through loss and tragedy, in
the awareness that there is One who does not give
up on us even when we have given up on ourselves.
Sometimes we are made aware that we are en-
countering a More-Than-Human-REAL OTHER when
in hours of solitude we have the deep sense of not
being alone. When like Isaiah in the temple we have
the sense of being called or summoned to service in
the world. When in the midst of our ordinary days
we come to the awareness that life is holy, there is
sanctity in existence. Yes, our own experience bears

witness to a *depth* and *grace* we sometimes overlook in the busyness of our lives.

So it was with some of the early Christians. They were living their usual day-by-day lives. They believed in God in a traditional way. But then Jesus came into their lives and "the lights came on." He opened to them an awareness of a wonder and depth and sanctity in their existence they had missed. They saw all things in a different way. So Paul exclaimed in interpreting the Christian experience, ". . . it is the God who said, 'Let light shine out of darkness,' who has shone in our hearts to give the light of the knowledge of the glory of God in the face of Christ. So we do not lose heart." (2 Corinthians 4:6, 16a)

When early Christian thinkers tried to bring together the chief convictions about God which were theirs, they said, "*God is known and experienced in at least three ways: as Creator, as Redeemer, as Life-Giving Spirit.*" That is the meaning of the doctrine of the Trinity.

Because God is Creator, creating still, the Christian sees creation as good. The natural world is not evil —it is of God. The seasons of life, the life-death cycle, the basic patterns of existence reveal a basic wisdom and goodness. "He has made everything beautiful in its time. " (Ecclesiastes 3:11) Man is a steward of the good earth, of the times and places and seasons of life.

Because God is Redeemer, redeeming still, the Christian understands that out of guilt can come forgiveness and new beginnings; out of suffering and loss and death can come new life; out of the sense of futility can come an awareness of purpose and meaning in life. The love revealed and mediated in Christ, brings healing and wholeness.

Because God is Life-Giving Spirit, still moving in the hearts and relationships of human beings, we may look to the future in expectation, knowing that God is with us in our todays—empowering, inspiring, leading us toward a community of truly matured and fulfilled human beings.

Yes, there is good news today about God. Deeper than the realm of the material, the tangible, the measurable is a Goodness and a Grace we comprehend only in part. But this Goodness and Grace, which we call God, is ever with us. The Christian understanding of God is disclosed in scripture, illumined by tradition, realized in experience and confirmed by reason. In the decision to walk in the light of God's presence and love we become alive in a new way.

I know my God to be—
What He knows me to be—
Alive.

Have you never wrestled with Him,
Never felt the muscle of His arm
In wind or tide or mountain-steep?
Never striving, drawn strength from Him?
Have you never matched minds with Him,
Never searched His secret in atom or in star,
Never felt the pain of infinite thinking?
Have you never been still,
Never been aware, before Him,
As He breathed an ideal into your soul?
Go to your God:
Ask Him to come to you
Alive.

(Author Unknown)

GOOD NEWS ABOUT PERSONS—
A DIGNITY YOU MAY HAVE DENIED

What mysterious creatures we are! We are problems to ourselves, to others, and perhaps—even to God. In an ancient and familiar story there is an account of the creation of the world and of man. We read, "And God saw everything that he had made, and behold, it was very good." (Genesis 1:31) However, if we turn over just a few chapters in the Book of Genesis we read this:

> The Lord saw that the wickedness of man was great in the earth, and that every imagination of the thoughts of his heart was only evil continually. And the Lord was sorry that he had made man on the earth, and it grieved him to his heart. (Genesis 6:5-6)

However, according to the biblical account God was not ready completely to give up on what he had started. At least a remnant was left to make something significant out of the human enterprise—a remnant maintaining life through the crisis of becoming the founder of a new humanity. In biblical thought the concept of a remnant keeps recurring. In our own time we are baffled by the human creature. He does such noble and creative and constructive things. But then he also does such ignoble, destructive, and cruel things. We are sometimes inclined to give up on ourselves. But the good news of the gospel is that *God does not give up on us even when we give up on ourselves.*

Even when we are condemning ourselves, rejecting ourselves, denying that our life has worth or future in it, there is a divine love that does not give up on us. Is that too good to be true? The gospel affirms that it is true. And countless human beings bear witness to the truth of it in their own experience.

George Fox, the founder of the Society of Friends, tells in his journal of his spiritual struggles as a young man. He visited a number of spiritual counselors, but to no avail. No one seemed to understand. One counselor suggested that he take up tobacco and sing Psalms. But, reported Fox, he did not like tobacco and he was in no shape to sing Psalms. Then he wrote these words, "There was none among them all that could speak to my condition."

His story did not stop there. He came at last to see how the Christian gospel did speak to his condition. He wrote, "Then the Lord gently led me along and let me see his love which was endless and eternal . . . this I know experimentally." His own experience convinced him that there is a divine caring that does not give up on us even when we give up on ourselves.

The Christian teaching is that human beings are unique creatures in the order of creation. They do, indeed, belong to the order of nature. But unlike inorganic things and lower forms of life, human beings have distinctive qualities and capacities.

When I look at thy heavens, the work of thy fingers,
the moon and the stars which thou hast established
what is man that thou art mindful of him,
and the son of man that thou dost care for him?
Yet thou hast made him little less than God,

and dost crown him with glory and honor."
(Psalm 8:3-5)

It is the Christian teaching that persons are more than cogs or clods. They are more than *things*. There is a spiritual dimension to human existence—and the purpose of life is to grow in this spiritual dimension. The human creature does not come "ready-made." Rather, the divine intention is that through the experiences of life persons might grow, might mature, might become centers of freedom and of love. The Christian interpretation is that human destiny is most truly fulfilled when the experiences and relationships and chapters of life contribute to a process of *becoming*.

The biblical writers kept using words which refer to the divine intention for man as that of becoming something new, growing, maturing. "If anyone is in Christ, he is a new creation. . . ." (2 Corinthians 5:17) "Speaking the truth in love, we are to grow up in every way into him who is the head, into Christ." (Ephesians 4:15)

Thus, the most important question about any human being is not "Where have you been?" but "In what direction are you going?"

According to Christian understanding we begin the journey of human life as infantile creatures—centered in self. If a newborn infant could speak adult words, he would be saying, "Give me what I want. I am the whole center of my concern." That is fine for an infant. But if one gets to be eighteen years of age, or forty-eight or eighty-eight, and has nothing more to say than, "Give me what I want. I am the center of everything"—he is in deep trouble. Life is designed for growth, moving into larger worlds of meaning and service, becoming centers of freedom and love. In Jesus Christ we are not only helped to understand what God is, but what human beings might become.

While Christian faith teaches that human beings are made for becoming, for growing, for maturing, it also faces the fact that there is that which blocks or gets in the way of human growth. Paul acknowledged that he was a problem to himself in these revealing words, ". . . I can will what is right, but I cannot do it. For I do not do the good I want, but the evil I do not want is what I do." (Romans 7:18-19) Sometimes we seem to be our own worst enemies. One of the familiar words long used to describe or illuminate the human situation is "sin." The word sin in a root sense means "to miss the mark." It comes from the language of archery. How often we miss the mark of what we might be. How often we are less than human or we try to be little gods; in either event we miss the mark of being truly human. How often, in our self-centeredness we rebel against the limitations which are part of life. How often we are estranged from the good earth, from other human beings, from God. How often we choose to regress rather than to grow; to exploit rather than to sustain and serve; to turn away from need rather than to assume responsibilities. How often we deny or distort the truth in order to enhance our own status. How often we overestimate our own virtues, powers, and achievements. How often our attitudes and actions reveal an inclination in the human heart which is not good. How often we resist the basic patterns of reality involving life and death, growing older, achieving growth of spirit through struggle and adversity. In these and other ways we miss the mark of our true selfhood. We become estranged from those processes and resources which bring life to its highest fulfillment.

We all need a clearer vision of the direction life can and ought to take. We all need the power and courage and motivation to move ahead, to grow, to aspire, to become. Apathy, laziness, the willingness to settle for a static kind of existence are indeed all sins of the spirit. Thus, there is no guarantee that life is going to unfold.

Sin has both individual and social dimensions. Groups, states, nations, institutions sometimes do damaging things to persons as persons. Insofar as they exploit persons, exercise dehumanizing influences, keep persons from realizing their finest possibilities they share in the guilt and evil of the world. No human being can escape from participation in some of the evil of the society in which he lives. To be human is to participate in both natural and social forces which hinder rather than enhance human growth. Sin as separation, as estrangement, as exploitive self-centeredness, as greed, as rebellion against the basic patterns of reality is a fact. Any realistic accounting of the human situation must take it into account.

But there is more to be said. Christian faith also affirms that man is "bearer of the image of God." Human beings have been given the capacity to think and feel and decide. Man has moral sensitivities; he aspires after ideals and goals; he longs to unite his life with other life and with God; he has been given the capacity to share in God's creating and renewing work.

If human life sometimes sinks to tragic depths, it also rises to heights of strength and nobility. We have all seen persons grow through adversity. We have seen individuals transformed through relationships with significant human beings. We have seen persons choose the hard right over the easy wrong. We have seen seemingly ordinary human beings use their time and talent and influence for great causes. We have seen faith and hope and love and courage in people. Persons are indeed wondrous creatures—capable of the worst and the best.

It is to this human creature, with his capacity for good and evil, for immaturity and maturity, for regression and progress, that the gospel comes. It speaks of the power of God in human life—a power to forgive and to change human hearts; a power to bring good out of what has seemed all tragedy; a power to help persons face up to the realities of their lives and to move to a higher life.

It is no accident that wherever the good news has been truly heard, there have been new efforts for educating persons, for rehabilitating persons, for setting people on their feet. John Wesley once wrote a letter to one of the Methodist societies which had expelled a member who had gone astray. Wesley wrote, "Let us set him on his feet once more." That is the Christian approach. To be Christian is to believe in persons and the power of God to enable persons to become new persons and to grow toward wholeness.

It is important for each of us to believe in the possibilities of his own life. We often tend to give up on ourselves. But Christian faith affirms the wonder of the human enterprise. God is in it. Your life is precious and important!

GOOD NEWS ABOUT LIFE—
A MEANING WAITING TO BE EXPERIENCED

> Living is a thing you do
> Now or never
> Which do you?

There is a spiritual hunger abroad in our world. In many ways many persons are saying, "Life ought to mean more than it does to the masses of men."

In a famous hymn Dr. Fosdick wrote of those who are "rich in things and poor in soul." Deep within many of us is the hunger for a deeper, more fulfilling quality of life. The endless, frantic search for *things* does not satisfy in the long run. One can achieve great possessions, great power, and great position and still be spiritually empty—less than human.

Erich Fromm has spoken of the widespread "underlying anxiety, depression, loneliness, boredom, and pain about the meaninglessness of life." In this situation persons sometimes seek escape. A special government study group has reported that alcoholism and alcohol abuse cost the nation fifteen billion dollars annually and blight the lives of millions of Americans. Many persons seek distraction through excessive television watching, overeating, spectator sports, drugs, relationships promising immediate intimacy, and not infrequently through religious movements which promise ecstatic experiences without responsibility for service to mankind. Astrology, spiritualism, witchcraft, cults of "consciousness expansion" appeal to increasing numbers of persons.

Perhaps we should not be surprised at this state of affairs. For a long time we have defined success in material terms and in terms of status. Much education has been education for this kind of success. We have defined the worthwhile life as a life of consuming *things* and satisfying our immediate desires. Isaac Watts expressed this approach to life as well as anyone:

> There are a number of us who creep
> Into this world, to eat and sleep,
> And know no reason why they're born
> But merely to consume the corn,
> Devour the cattle, fowl and fish,
> And leave behind an empty dish.
> The crows and raven do the same,
> Unlucky birds of hateful name;
> Ravens or crows might fill their place
> And swallow corn and carcasses.
> Then, if their tombstone when they die
> Contain no flattery nor lie
> There's nothing better will be said
> Than that, they've eaten all their bread
> Drank up their drink, and gone to bed.

Barbara Ward, the economist, has said that a nation which spends more per capita on advertising than on education has lost its way to the future. The priorities which we set in terms of our expenditure of money, time, talent provide a clue to the "crisis of soul" and crisis of meaning in which we now find ourselves. Under these circumstances we are discovering that among many persons there is a new openness to the ancient wisdom that man does not live by bread alone. Just as our physical natures require food, so our minds and hearts and spirits require nourishment. The finer feelings, the nobler aspirations, the profounder visions, the deeper sensitivities all are essential if man is to achieve true wholeness. The hunger for wholeness is very real in today's world. Basically our quest is a religious one. In the seventeenth century Meister Eckhart wrote, "Know that, by nature, every creature seeks to become like God. Nature's intent is neither food nor drink nor clothing, nor comfort, nor anything else in which God is left out. Whether you like it or not, whether you know it or not, secretly nature seeks, hunts, tries to ferret out the track on which God may be found." Beneath the surface of our lives we are restless until we find a harmonious relationship with the source of all life. We seek a vision of and a oneness with the Whole of which we are parts. There is a deep prompting to go beyond what and where we now are to a fulfillment which yields joy, serenity, wisdom, creativity, and power. Consciously or unconsciously we are seekers after God. May Sarton has expressed the need many of us are feeling:

Return to the deep sources; nothing less
Will nourish the torn spirit
The angry mind: and from the ultimate duress
Pierced with the breath of anguish, speak for love.

It is good news that there are persons who demonstrate the reality of "a more excellent way." There are persons whose lives make the gospel believable. In such lives we see transformations of mind and heart and spirit. We see guilt-ridden, fear-ridden lives made new. We see lives which have gone to pieces achieve wholeness. We see lives which had lost meaning come to have purpose and direction. One person who had experienced devastation of mind and spirit and who had then found a new life in the faith and fellowship of the church, wrote:

I climb, who was a clod,
I run, whose steps were slow;
I reap the very wheat of God
Who once had none to sow.

It is a wondrous thing when we meet a person who has come alive in a new way. To move from deadness of spirit to the kindling sense of the wonder of life; to move from immature self-centeredness to great loyalties and love of persons; to move from a sense of worthlessness to the awareness of the sanctity of all lives—including one's own—this is indeed a miracle of new birth. Christian faith affirms that he who is in Christ is truly a new creation. This affirmation is not only theory; it has been and is an accomplished fact in many lives. It is a possibility for those who truly seek it.

Reinhold Niebuhr once wrote that more effective than any argument is the witness of a life made new. He said, ". . . the only effective witness of the truth of Christ is a life in which the anxieties and fears of life have been overcome, including the fear of death; in which the prison of self-love, of preoccupation with the self, its interests and securities, has been broken so that the self can live in 'love, joy and peace.' That is, be so free of anxieties as to enter creatively into the lives of others." Perhaps no one ever fully achieves these victories of the spirit. But there are enough persons who have achieved them in significant measure, and enough persons who are growing in "the fruits of the spirit" that we more readily find the gospel to be believable.

The hymn writer wrote of the wonder of God's creative power in the world of nature about us. More wonderful still, he said, is God's working in human hearts and relationships, bringing new life:

We've seen thy glory like a mantle spread
O'er hill and dale in saffron flame and red;
But in the eyes of men redeemed and free,
A splendor greater yet while serving thee.

The new life of which Christian faith speaks is grounded in personal experience of God. Rufus Jones, the Quaker leader who combined in a remarkable way concern for the inner life of the spirit with a concern for service to those in need, once spoke of "an immediate, experimental knowledge of God." He went on to say, "One of the most significant effects of experiences of this sort is the resulting deepening of life and a marked increase in joy. . . . The person concerned goes down to deeper foundations for the structure of life. . . . There comes that marked depth of calm and serenity." He also said, "To some the truth of God never comes closer than a logical conclusion. . . . To the (person of faith) he becomes real in the same sense that experienced beauty is real, or the feel of spring is real, or that summer sunlight is real—he has been found, he has been met, he is present." The life which is truly worth living goes deeper than the surface level of things. It is in touch with the divine ground and source of all being—God. It is not taken out of the time stream, but it is in tune with the eternal in the midst of time.

William James once said that religion is the relaxation of the effort to be self-sufficient. The person of faith knows that he does not need to carry all the load alone. He has his responsibilities, but God is at the heart of a life in a sustaining and empowering way.

To know the reality and presence of God *experimentally* puts everything in a different light. Life is undergirded. Life is more truly alive. One does not walk alone. One has a new kind of relationship with all creatures. The world is wonderful in a way we had not realized before. One is more free to accept himself, to see the best in others, to affirm this very day and hour. One is more free to go beyond the past and to accept God's offer of new opportunities, new relationships, new chapters. One feels what the poet had in mind in these words:

> And through and over everything
> A sense of glad awakening.

Ordinary things, routine experiences, the people around us come to have a new kind of meaning when life is lived in the sense of God's presence and love. Our own resources are undergirded by resources from beyond ourselves. The future calls in a new way. Problems are real, pain is real, tragedy is real, struggles of the soul are real—but all these things are seen and experienced in a different way. Life, we know, has depth and purpose and we are not in it all alone. "For I am sure that neither death, nor life . . . nor any thing else in all creation, will be able to separate us from the love of God in Christ Jesus our Lord." (Romans 8:38-39)

The letters of Paul to the early Christian churches are living witnesses to one man's experience of God—a transforming experience mediated through Jesus Christ. In his encounter with Jesus Christ and in his response of faith and commitment, Paul experienced entrance into a new life. He knew himself to be forgiven, to be made free as he had never been free before. He came under a higher control, he was empowered, he was called into service. Out of his experience of new life in the spirit he exclaimed, "I am not ashamed of the gospel: it is the power of God for salvation to every one who has faith." (Romans 1:16) In interpreting the new life to the Galatians Paul said, "You were called to freedom, brethren; only do not use your freedom as an opportunity for the flesh, but through love be servants of one another." (Galatians 5:13)

After years of inner self-rejection, conflict and turmoil Martin Luther came to know that peace and freedom of soul cannot come through man's own feverish efforts alone. It was only as he relinquished some long-cherished idols and placed his trust in the God whose love was revealed in Christ, that he came to know true freedom and new life. Like Paul he found joy and gratitude in the redemptive power which laid hold on him. Ten years after his conversion he wrote these words:

> For faith through the merit of Christ obtaineth the Holy Spirit, which Spirit doth make new hearts . . . doth excite and inflame our heart, that it may do those things willingly of love which the law commandeth . . . yea doth so embolden the heart of the true believer, that trusting to have God on his side, he is not afraid to oppose himself alone against all creatures.
>
> (Preface to the Romans)

On May 24, 1738 a troubled soul heard those very words read—probably in this same translation. He felt his heart strangely warmed. He went forth from that meeting on Aldersgate Street to live as a new person and to lead in a great movement of religious awakening. This was the experience of John Wesley.

Each person makes his own religious pilgrimage. Details of our religious histories vary. For some persons the entrance into the new life of the spirit is attended by high moments of ecstasy. For others it comes more quietly and gradually. But always there is the relaxation of the effort to be self-sufficient. Always there is the placing of one's trust in God, whose ways may not always be our ways. Always it involves the readiness and desire to walk in the new light which has come. Always there is a new awareness that life has direction and depth and purpose. New life in the spirit is a life of "growth in grace." It is marked by a movement of life from fear and anxiety to a deepening trust (faith); it is marked by a movement of life from apathy and despair to more creative hope; it is marked by movement from self-centeredness and indifference to the need of others, to a profounder quality of loving. This new life of freedom from the past and openness to the future is what Paul called the "more excellent way." It is a way of personal fulfillment. It is a way of creative involvement in the world. It is a way of trust and celebration—with all life lived in praise of God. It is a new life in Christ.

God gives to each of us a measure of freedom in choosing his own way of life. If we choose to go along pretty much as in the past, that is for us to decide. But if we wish to look more deeply into the claims of Christian faith, that also is for us to decide. No one can force us when it comes to the deep things of the spirit.

The rest of this book is intended for those who are of a mind to carry further their own inner search for a more fulfilling way of life. It is for those who are attracted by the Christian vision of reality and the Christian vision of what human life can mean. It is for those who in the depths of their beings would be whole persons in a whole world.

GOOD NEWS ABOUT OURSELVES—
SOME DECISIONS WE CAN MAKE

One of the most famous conversations recorded in the New Testament is that between Jesus and Nicodemus. We are told that Nicodemus, a man of standing among the Pharisees, came to Jesus by night. (John 3:1 ff.) Apparently he was seeking some deeper understanding, some better way of life, which he thought Jesus might bring to him. It was in this conversation that Jesus talked about the possibility and the necessity of being born anew. "Truly, truly, I say to you, unless one is born anew, he cannot see the kingdom of God."

This kind of talk bewildered Nicodemus. "How can a man be born when he is old?" he asked.

Probably many of us, at some time or other, have thought we would like to start life all over again. We think of mistakes we have made and of opportunities we have missed. Yes, there is something to be said for the idea of starting over again. But then we are inclined to dismiss such thoughts as being unrealistic; we settle back into our familiar routine. Deep down inside we are not at all sure that we want to be changed. If only things could be better without our really being changed!

But Jesus has reminded us that we are only deceiving ourselves if we wish for a better life without being open to some changes within ourselves. We cannot stand still and move ahead at the same time!

Jesus pointed out that there is much of mystery in the coming of new life—in being born anew. Man cannot manipulate the spirit of God. Jesus said, "The wind blows where it wills, and you hear the sound of it, but you do not know whence it comes or whither it goes; so it is with every one who is born of the Spirit." (John 3:8)

Yet, the coming of new life is not *wholly* God's doing. If man cannot manipulate God neither does God manipulate man. God has given man power of choice and decision and commitment. In writing to the Corinthians Paul said of the church, "I planted, Apollos watered, but God gave the growth." (1 Corinthians 3:6) So it is in the life of the spirit. God is the ultimate giver of life and new life. But persons have their responsibilities in God's purposes for growth.

William Hocking once observed that a very slight shift in the set of the rudder of a ship at the outset of a voyage makes a great difference in the point of arrival. The New Testament says, "Look at the ships also; though they are so great and are driven by strong winds, they are guided by a very small rudder wherever the will of the pilot directs." (James 3:4)

Each one of us has a voice in determining what direction our lives will take. The direction of our wishing, willing, intending, aspiring is important. We cannot determine the precise details of our lives. There is much of mystery about how many things will come out. But we do have a voice in determining the direction our lives take, *beginning where we are*. If we decide that we want to go along pretty much as we have been going, that is the way it will be. But if we are sincere in saying that we wish to move beyond where we are, that is also a possibility.

Good faith in seeking a new life in Christ involves the making of some decisions. They are not easy decisions. They come at a cost. But multitudes have found that the cost is really very little in comparison to the riches of the life which is truly life. Let us note some of the decisions which we can make if we choose to.

1. The decision honestly to assess our present situation. Are we basically satisfied to live out the rest of our days according to the pattern "to which we have become accustomed"? Or are we sincere in the desire to find deeper meanings in life than we have known? *What do we really want?*

2. The decision to take risks and to discard something of the old in order that we might go on from where we are. To grow is to outgrow—that means leaving some things behind. In order to be born to some new things we must die to some old things. There must be a beginning somewhere—and that beginning may involve leaving behind some old idols, some old masks, some old evasions, some old pretenses. Are we really ready to risk a future which is not guaranteed?

3. The decision to walk in the light of the gospel—sincerely seeking to order our lives in the light of our best understanding of what the gospel is saying to us. This is an act of commitment of the greatest importance. It means finding a directing center for our lives. It means making decisions, not simply in terms of what is pleasant, but in terms of what the gospel summons us to do. Our readiness to make this decision is one of the acid tests of our sincerity in relation to the Christian life. Paul wrote, ". . . let your manner of life be worthy of the gospel of Christ." (Philippians 1:27a) The decision of which we

are now speaking involves much more than doing the Christian thing *when it suits our convenience*. The decision to order our lives in the light of the gospel may involve reordering our priorities, rethinking how we are going to invest our time, talent, and money, seriously questioning whether we have really been giving God a chance in our lives.

4. The decision sincerely to be open to the leadings of God's spirit. How often we try to make all the decisions. How often we assume that we have failed if things do not work out just as we had planned. The Christian life begins when we sincerely place our trust in God, commit our lives to God's will as that is disclosed in Jesus Christ, gladly yielding our lives to purposes which may be greater than our own, to destinies which we cannot possibly see with our limited vision. "Trust in the Lord with all your heart. . . . In all your ways acknowledge him, and he will make straight your paths." (Proverbs 3:5-6)

5. The decision to be open to the possibility that God can work important changes in your life. How skeptical we are! Just one week before the successful flight of the Wright brothers the *New York Times* said this about another plane builder: "We hope that Professor Langley will not put his substantial greatness as a scientist in further peril by continuing to waste his time, and the money involved, in further airship experiments. Life is short, and he is capable of services to humanity incomparably greater than can be expected from trying to fly." In similar vein we sometimes doubt that the human spirit can really take wings moving into new worlds of experience. A young man, troubled in spirit, contemplated a tree one winter day. He thought of the changes which would take place in that tree with the coming of

spring—new life, new leaves, new beauty. Under the inspiration of that moment he exclaimed, "If God can work such wonders in an ordinary tree, what wonders could He work in my life if I were truly open to Him?" That young man made the decision truly to be open to God. He came to be known as Brother Lawrence, with whose life we associate the devotional classic *The Practice of the Presence of God*.

6. The decision to expose ourselves to persons and groups and writings through which we will be strengthened, encouraged, and guided in our search for a new life in the spirit. In the deep things of the spirit we cannot lift ourselves by our own bootstraps. We need the undergirding of the "the fellowship of kindred minds." There are great writings, within and outside the Bible, which inform and inspire. There are persons and groups in whose fellowship our spirits will be nurtured. One of the powers with which we have been endowed is the power to have a voice in determining what influences will have a chance at us. Great music, great literature, great personalities are all waiting to minister to us. Christian groups devoted to undergirding one another in the life of faith are available, or can be formed.

7. The decision to utilize "means of grace" through which our relationship with God is deepened and nurtured. Regular worship, prayer, devotional meditation, the sacraments contribute greatly to the growth of the life in God. But little can happen without the personal decision to make the "means of grace" a regular part of our lives. As Joseph Fort Newton put it, "We must take time, take pains, have a plan, form spiritual habits, if we are to keep our souls alive; and now is the time to begin."

8. The decision to try to mean something to some other person or persons on their spiritual quests. Is it surprising to suppose that you might mean something to someone else in these matters? Try it! Simply sharing your own interests and concerns may open doors you never suspected were there. We talk to each other about so many trivial things. How tragic that we so seldom talk to each other about the ultimately important concerns. In helping others we are helped. And in being open to the concerns of others, they will be helped. We all need to be needed!

9. The decision to seek the presence, the power, and the leadings of God in our daily experiences. How often we think of the experience of God as being something separate from the normal experiences of life. We seek God away from our work and human relationships and varied responsibilities. Yet, as Moses discovered, the very ground on which we stand may be holy ground. In the next section of this book we shall consider this matter in greater detail. At this point, let us simply note that God gives us life in the body, in this world, in human relationships for spiritual ends. We are created *to become* more truly human, more truly bearers of the image of God. And this spiritual formation, this divine becoming, occurs in the very midst of the day by day experiences of life. Each day can be dedicated to the glory of God in the manner of our living it.

Here, then, are nine important decisions we can make—if we choose to. Which are we prepared to make? A journey of a thousand miles begins with a single step.

PART THREE

THE EXPERIENCE OF GOD

The Boy: "Tell me, what is the wind?"
The Old Sailor: "I don't quite know how to describe the wind, but I will teach you how to hoist a sail."

"The majority of men never experience the spiritual life; they never experience the qualitative encounter with the divine." Soren Kierkegaard

"The modern world has lost God and is seeking him." Alfred North Whitehead

"You will seek me and find me; when you seek me with all your heart." Jeremiah 29:13

"A Christian man ought to be so disposed and prepared as to reflect that he has to do with God every moment of his life." John Calvin

"If a man believes and knows God,
    he can no longer ask,
'What is the meaning of my life?'
    But by believing
he actually lives the meaning of his life."
                                    (Karl Barth)

YOUR OWN EXPERIENCE OF GOD

"Religion," said William James, "exists in some persons as a dull habit, and in others as an acute fever."

The New Testament speaks of those "holding the form of religion but denying the power of it." (2 Timothy 3:5)

With obvious reference to the Timothy statement John Wesley described the early Methodist societies as "a company of men having the form and seeking the power of godliness.

Statements such as these remind us of what is obvious—one can go through certain religious forms without necessarily experiencing religion as a transforming reality.

Many of us were taught, many years ago, about how God spoke to certain eminent persons of the past. We were asked to learn about some *other* person's experience of God. Too seldom were we told that religion becomes alive and real only in terms of our own, personal experiences of God. Too seldom were we given help in discerning the divine presence in our own lives.

Yet, God is available to each and every person. The religious experiences of no two persons are identical. Each of us makes his own religious pilgrimage. As we speak of these matters with other persons we are likely to learn that we have much in common. But God becomes transformingly real only when God is known in the midst of our own personal lives.

Someone once observed that no other person can take your bath for you, die your death for you, or make your basic commitments for you. Similarly no other persons can have your experiences of God for you. Secondhand religion is not enough.

Most persons have more spiritual capital with which to work than they realize. Samuel Miller must have had something like this mind when he wrote, ". . . let your soul speak for itself. . . . Quit dressing your soul in somebody else's piety. Your soul is not a pauper. Let it live its own life."

Someone may well ask, "But what do you mean by an experience of God?" Perhaps this person goes on to say, "I have known some persons who have had very special experiences which they called 'religious experiences.' I cannot honestly say that I have ever had such an experience. Does this mean that I have never had nor can ever have experience of God?"

This is a searching kind of question and we must deal with it as honestly as we can. It is true that some persons have what might be called "peak experiences" which stand out clearly from the normal on-going experiences of life. These experiences may involve special illumination, the sense of divine presence, release from distressing worry or guilt, ecstatic feeling, empowerment from beyond oneself. That such experiences are real there is no doubt. That profound transformations of life sometimes attend such experiences there is no doubt. But it does not follow from this that all experiences of God are of this sort. Nor does it follow that all "religious experiences" are of equal meaning and value in the growth of the spiritual life.

Questions of this sort rose in the early Christian church at Corinth. What are the marks of the working of the spirit? What is the Christian's experience of God? Paul addressed himself to these matters. The church was being divided over them and he recognized the importance of bringing certain norms or standards to bear on claims that this or that experience was the "highest" or "supreme" experience of God.

As we read Paul's various writings it becomes clear that he thought at least two questions should be asked of any experience which claimed to be a *Christian* experience of God: (1) Is it edifying? (2) Does it express, nurture, or call forth Christian love?

In discussing the matter of speaking in tongues Paul wrote, "Let all things be done for edification." (1 Corinthians 14:26b) Paul uses the term edify in the root sense of encouraging, building, building up. He is concerned with building up fellow-believers and building up the church. ". . . in church I would rather speak five words with my mind, in order to instruct others, than ten thousand words in a tongue. For God is not a God of confusion but of peace." (1 Corinthians 14:19, 33)

In writing to the same Corinthian group Paul insisted that it is love that builds up. (1 Corinthians 8:1) In his classic "love chapter" Paul said "If I speak in the tongues of men and of angels, but have not love, I am a noisy gong or a clanging symbol. So faith, hope, love abide; but the greatest of these is love." (1 Corinthians 13:1, 13)

In writing to the Galatians Paul put it this way: ". . . the fruit of the Spirit is love, joy, peace, patience, kindness, goodness, faithfulness, gentleness, self-control; against such there is no law." (Galatians 5:22)

Statements such as these make it clear that Paul believed that there are norms and standards which must be applied to any claims that a particular experience is an experience of God in a Christian sense. He believed that some persons may be entirely sincere and even enthusiastic about their religious experiences—but still miss the point of Christian understanding. Thus, in writing to the Romans he spoke of those who "have a zeal for God but it is not enlightened." (Romans 10:2)

Religious experiences, according to Paul, are not to be judged simply on the basis of whether someone finds them enjoyable or ecstatic. It must be asked: Do they reflect the deepest understanding of God and God's active presence as that is made known in Christ? Do they issue in a life of spiritual growth marked by faith and hope and love? Do they go beyond a purely subjective, individualistic experience to participation in "the body of Christ" as a serving-witnessing fellowship? Paul strongly felt that the Christian life involves thought, feeling, commitment. Authentic Christian experience nurtures wholeness of life.

Throughout the nineteen centuries of Christian history sincere seekers after Christian truth have pondered the wonder and the mysteries of God's life in the souls and relationships of persons. No single experience is the full measure of God's presence with man. No single experience encompasses the whole range of man's experiences of God.

The old order changeth, yielding place to new
And God fulfills himself in many ways.

(Alfred Tennyson)

God comes to man at various times, in various settings, in various ways. Through the centuries it has become clearer that if we are to talk of religious experience within a Christian frame of reference, we need to take four things into account: the testimony of scripture, tradition, experience, and reason. If sincerely we seek to be taught and sensitized through scripture, tradition, experience, and reason *within the fellowship of Christian persons,* we will almost certainly move toward truth in relation to man's experiences of God.

To believe in God in a Christian sense is to believe in the creator God—creating, judging, providing still. It is to believe in the redeeming God—redeeming, healing, reconciling still, through the love of Christ reveals and mediates. It is to believe in the empowering, prodding, guiding, inspiring, sanctifying God—whose active presence sets us to the life-long task of "grateful and gracious living." The experience of God, in a Christian sense, involves one's personal experience of this living God—creating, redeeming, transforming, inspiring, summoning to service!

He to whom the presence and power of God is experientially real comes to a depth of assurance about some fundamental matters, even though there may still be "dark nights of the soul." He is assured that there is more to life than the material, the tangible, the measurable and the controllable. He is assured that mankind is not alone in an uncaring universe. He is assured that in life and in death we are dealing with the Eternal Thou, ever worthy of our trust and devotion. He is assured that we live and die in relation to the One who judges all our lesser loyalties, who is the very ground of our existence, who sometimes rebukes us but also offers healing and forgiveness, who calls us into a truly human existence, who is the inspiration of our deepest faith and hope and love. He is assured that mankind is born for a higher destiny than that of clod or cog or consumer. Persons are born to bear the image of God—in grateful, celebrative, co-creating, serving stewardship. He is assured that in all times it is appropriate to pray: "Direct us, O Lord, in all our doings with thy most gracious favor, and further us with thy continual help, that in all our works, begun, continued, and ended in thee, we may glorify thy holy name, through Jesus Christ, our Lord."

Whence comes the assurance of one's personal experience of God? Often painful struggle is part of it—struggle of reason, of conscience, of decision. Sometimes periods of "dryness" and unrewarding effort are part of it. Sometimes fellowship with fellow searchers is part of it. Sometimes high moments of insight and inspiration are part of it. Sometimes hours of doubt are part of it. But almost always there is a meeting with a person or persons to whom God is transformingly real. And to the Christian, most important of all, is the meeting with Jesus Christ (who comes to us in many forms) but always bringing the word of judgment and the word of grace. Even as he calls us and our ways to account, he offers new life.

THE EXPERIENCE OF GOD—
IN HIGH MOMENTS OF
DISCOVERY AND ILLUMINATION

Life sometimes brings "rare best moments" when we experience discovery, illumination, wholeness, deliverance from guilt and fear, a profound sense of goodness of life.

That, at least, is the testimony of many persons. To be sure, not all persons claim to have had such experiences. Among those who do, there is variation in the frequency and the intensity of the experiences. But many persons do bear witness to such experiences, saying that life is seen more clearly, and lived more meaningfully, in the light of such hours of discovery and illumination.

Experiences of discovery and illumination are not always religious in character—at least in the usual meaning of religious. Some persons report "flashes of insight" which they have experienced. A distinguished biologist tells of working in the laboratory on a particular problem when suddenly there came a flash of insight which he needed and which opened up a solution to the problem. He refers to this as "the A-HA!" phenomenon. In the midst of struggling with a problem one exclaims "A-HA!" There has been a breakthrough. In a similar vein we think of Archimedes running through the streets shouting "Eureka." (I have found it!)

An eminent psychiatrist speaks of "the experience of an essential inner change in the human personality, achieved through a succession of moments of deeply moving and often painful discovery of truths about oneself.'' He then speaks of the emancipation which sometimes comes when one, through these discoveries, is made free to enter life with less of evasion and fear. One is alive in a new way.

The poet Keats described the opening up of mind and spirit which came to him through the reading of Chapman's *Homer*.

> Then felt I like some watcher of the skies
> When a new planet swims upon his ken.

So we might go on, recalling persons who have experienced "breakthroughs" of the mind and spirit. All life has been different by virtue of the discoveries which have been made, the illuminations which have come.

But now we are primarily interested in high moments of discovery and illumination which are more distinctively religious in character. The Bible tells of many persons whose vision of life and whose sense of personal destiny was wrapped up with some transforming moment or moments. It has happened in many ways: a burning bush for Moses, a cry in the night for Samuel, seeing a man sell himself into slavery for Amos, an unfaithful wife for Hosea, a potter's wheel for Jeremiah, a sanctuary experience for Isaiah, a blinding light for Paul.

Through the centuries of Christian history it has continued to happen in many ways: through the witness of some person or persons who have spoken of how God has moved in their lives, through participation in a group searching-sharing persons, through experiences of worship in which all life has been lifted into the presence of God, through a call for help, through some experience of cleansing of beauty, through an experience of being loved.

It is understandable that many persons think first of such high moments of discovery and illumination and transfiguration when they would speak of the experience of God.

It was in a moment of awe and wonder that the Psalmist exclaimed, "O Lord, our Lord, how majestic is thy name in all the earth!" (Psalm 8:1) It was in a moment of profound gratitude for the deliverance he had experienced that the words were spoken, "He drew me up from the desolate pit, out of the miry bog, and set my feet upon a rock, making my steps secure. He put a new song in my mouth." (Psalm 40:2-3a)

It was in the joy and meaning of a new life in Christ that Paul wrote, ". . . thanks be to God, who in Christ always leads us in triumph. It is the God who said 'Let light shine out of darkness,' who has shone in our hearts to give the light of the knowledge of the glory of God in the face of Christ." (2 Corinthians 2:14; 4:6)

Through the centuries of Christian history there have been those who have witnessed to high moments in which they have experienced the presence of God in and around them, have known his love in a transforming way, have been made aware of a glory in the commonplace and sanctity in all existence, have been both summoned to service and empowered to do what they were called to do.

The philosopher-mathematician Pascal uttered just one word in such a high moment of discovery and illumination: "Fire!"

The poet Wordsworth wrote:

> While with an eye made quiet by the power

61

Of harmony, and the deep power of joy,
We see into the life of things. . . ."

Dag Hammarskjold tells of his deep hunger for a sense of meaning in his life. Then, ". . . at some moment I did answer *Yes* to Someone—or Something—and from that hour I was certain that existence is meaningful and that, therefore, my life in self-surrender, had a goal."

George Fox told of his discouraging search for spiritual help, when no one seemed to be able to speak to his condition. But then he reports in his journal, "While I was in that condition, it was opened unto me by the eternal light and power, and I therein clearly saw that all was done and to be done by Christ."

Rufus Jones has written: "What is true of love is just as true of God and the world of spiritual realities. There come high moments when we find ourselves where we know we *belong,* when the Beyond is here and the Yonder is present. These eternal moments take the soul to the very heart of reality."

Such high moments and hours of discovery and illumination and communion are indeed real. The Christian believes that God is in them, their source and inspiration. Such experiences bring a deepened assurance, new hope, and a new quality of caring about people and things—and life itself. One knows that life is not all on the surface; it has depth. One knows that one does not walk alone; God is ever with us. One knows that life cannot be measured by clocks and calendars alone; the eternal is in the midst of the temporal.

In hours of fatigue and discouragement, and self-rejection, and loneliness, and failure; in hours of loss and guilt and emptiness of spirit; in hours when life seems nothing but wearisome routine, it is a blessing to have high moments of discovery and illumination to remember and on which to draw. As an old man Whittier reflected on the things for which he was most grateful. Among other things, he spoke of "the fountains by the way." So, life's high moments are like fountains by the way which have not only refreshed our spirits, but have brought newness of life and purpose.

Henry Thoreau said, "Every man is asked to make his life . . . worthy of the contemplation of his most elevated hours." Life cannot be simply a series of "mountain-top experiences." But life can be lived in recollection of those rare best moments and hours when it has been given us to see more clearly, to believe more deeply, to trust more sincerely, and to love God and man more completely. Life can be lived in the awareness that God comes to us in many ways in many settings. We need to be open to his coming.

And life should be lived in the awareness that no experience of special discovery and illumination should be a stopping point. The Christian life is a life of going on and growing on. The spirit's "rare best moments" are not only something to remember; they are points from which to go on into a life which is truly being perfected in understanding, in love, and in service.

We do well to recall the words of John Calvin: "A Christian man ought to be so disposed and prepared as to reflect that he has to do with God every moment of his life." The experience of God awaits us in *every* situation. The following chapters will endeavor to explore this theme.

THE EXPERIENCE OF GOD—IN ORDINARY DAYS

God gives us the gift of life one day at a time.

Each day is a life in miniature. Each waking in the morning is a new birth. Each going to sleep at night involves a little death—the concluding of a segment of life. It is over. And in the hours between our waking and going to sleep there is the opportunity to seek and find and express those values of the heart and mind and spirit which we would have characterize our lives as a whole.

Life is the sum total of our individual days. The glory of a life well lived is the glory of single days well lived. The Psalmist rejoiced in the gift of a single day and prayed that each day might be lived to the glory of God. "This is the day which the Lord has made; let us rejoice and be glad in it." (Psalm 118:24) "So teach us to number our days that we may get a heart of wisdom." (Psalm 90:12)

Our experiences of God are associated with individual days. The God "in whom we live and move and have our being" is present in the flow of events— in days like today. Any knowledge of God and any personal experience of God which may ever be ours will be within some day or days.

And yet, some days are so ordinary. Some days are so routine. Some days are so commonplace. How can we possibly speak of the experience of God in ordinary days? Is God not most truly known in special days, in high moments of discovery and illumination?

Sometimes we forget that routine is inevitably part of an orderly universe. Without it we would have chaos rather than cosmos. If there were nothing but novelty we would soon yearn for a routine and some repetition. Phillips Brooks said, "Routine is a terrible master, but she is a servant whom we can hardly do without. Routine as a law is deadly. Routine as a resource in the temporary exhaustion of impulse and suggestion is often our salvation." If God is truly present in the basic structures and patterns and processes of reality, then perhaps he is present in very ordinary days!

John Keble, the hymn-writer, expressed his feelings about these matters in these lines:

> The trivial round, the common task,
> Will furnish all we ought to ask,
> If on our daily course our mind
> Be set to hallow all we find.

Hallowing all we find! Martin Buber expressed a similar thought: "God speaks to every man through the life He gives him again and again. . . . There is no true human share of holiness without the hallowing of the everyday."

Let us consider some of the ways in which our relationship with God may be expressed and deepened *in very ordinary days*. For one thing, each day affords the opportunity to accept God's permission to leave some things behind us. Is it not tragic how we sometimes become enslaved to the past? Sometimes we drag the past with us unnecessarily. Sometimes we seem to organize our thinking and living around some past mistake, some past misfortune, some past loss, some past injustice.

Yet, the gospel assures us that God keeps offering us newness of life. We cannot erase the past. But, by the grace of God, we can go beyond it. God is a God of new beginnings. On even ordinary days we can demonstrate our readiness to accept God's offer to go beyond where we have been.

Again, ordinary days provide the opportunity to break through dullness of vision and spirit to see that ordinary days are not so ordinary after all! G. K. Chesterton observed that "the world will never starve for want of wonders, but only for want of wonder." In similar vein Emerson said, "If the stars should appear but one night in a thousand years, how would men believe and adore and preserve for many generations the remembrance of the City of God which had been shown." In the food we eat, in the tools we use, in the conversations we share, in the services rendered by persons around us and in our community there is so much of wonder. How anyone can be bored in a world like this is hard to understand. Each day affords the opportunity to "wake up" in mind and heart and sensitivity—to the wonders which are a part of very ordinary days.

Ordinary days are just as good as other days for making some of the basic decisions which are involved in the Christian life. The decision to look honestly at one's values and priorities; the decision to be more truly open to God; the decision to seek a deeper understanding of what it is to commit one's life to Jesus Christ and the life he offers; the decision to find time for the "means of grace"; the decision to try to be more sensitive to the thoughts and feelings and concerns of other people; the decision to live this day, this hour, this situation as a disciple of Christ—all these important decisions can be made on very ordinary days. But in the making of them, we discover that something of wonder has taken place. The day has been hallowed. "This is the day which the Lord has made; let us rejoice and be glad in it!"

No matter what the day may be like externally, we can live it so that we express those values of heart and mind and spirit which we would have characterize our lives as a whole. Would we be just and kind and understanding? We can be those things today. Would we speak the word of encouragement and hope? We can speak those words today. Would we be open to goodness and beauty and truth? We can express that openness today. Would we pause from time to time to reflect on the wonder of God's presence in us and around us? That can be a part of today's experience. Would we keep learning and would we keep growing? There is no day, however ordinary, which does not provide opportunity for that. *Whatever you want your life to mean can be expressed this very day!*

Mrs. Rena Mary Taylor served in the Colorado legislature for a number of years. She stood for good legislation which would help persons. She was mindful of the needs of the less fortunate and the estranged. Well along in years she suffered a stroke and a heart attack in quick succession. Slowly regaining strength she wrote these lines in a Christmas letter: "During this just passed year, which was so nearly my last on earth, I have learned many lessons. I now breathe a prayer of gratitude to God at each morning's dawn that He has given me another day of opportunity for living and learning. . . . Today I believe I am aware as never before of the value of a day of life. How little we really make of days of living and the years God has given us to live, to learn and grow." The hallowing of the every day!

Perhaps the day on which you are reading this page seems like an ordinary day. Would it not be a wonderful day if it might mean a moving beyond a certain dimness of spirit to the awareness that there is a Depth which speaks to your depth? Would it not be a wonderful day if in the depths of your being you came to know that while you cannot erase the past, God permits you to go beyond it? You are free to do that. Would it not be a wonderful day if it were given you to know that although you may have given up on yourself, there is a Love which has not given up on you? Would it not be a wonderful day if you came to the realization that you can mean something to someone else? Would it not be a wonderful day if, out of all the difficult things you have known, you might begin to breathe more deeply, to hope more sincerely, to feel more freely, and to love more sincerely? If this could be, today would not really be an ordinary day at all. It would be a day in which you have experienced God.

THE EXPERIENCE OF GOD—
IN DARK NIGHTS OF THE SOUL

Several years ago I was writing a book on *The Inner Life*. A wise physician friend asked, "Will you include a chapter for me?" I asked what he had in mind. He replied, "Tell the people that it is all right to have feelings."

How important it is to understand that it is all right to have feelings! They are God-given. Without the capacity for feeling we would be less than human. Yet, many of life's most difficult problems revolve around our feelings—about ourselves, about other persons, about experiences, about life. We would not want it said of us that we were unfeeling persons. On the other hand, how often we have wished to be relieved of the pain of some emotions. The ancient words are relevant in every generation: "He who is slow to anger is better than the mighty, and he who rules his spirit than he who takes a city." (Proverbs 16:32)

In this section of our study we shall consider the painful feelings which attend two common experiences —those of doubting and of being depressed. It may seem strange indeed to talk about experiencing God in the midst of doubt and depression. But before dismissing this as an incredible notion, let us look more deeply into the possible meanings of these experiences. After all, the deeper significance of any experience is not whether it is pleasant or unpleasant, easy or difficult, but what it comes to mean to us. What do the experiences of doubt and depression come to do to us and in us?

It is painful to know that there is so much we cannot know. Someone once defined education as the process of becoming increasingly aware of one's ignorance. The more we learn about some things the more we realize that we have only scratched the surface of understanding. We must live with much mystery about many matters. It is no virtue to claim to know more than we really do.

Religion, in the face of great mystery, is often more of an attitude than an answer. The attitude of trust is more important than conjectures as to what *might* be. One of the greatest Christian theologians who ever lived was Augustine (354-430). He once said, "If you have been able to understand it, it is not God that you contemplate." He was a great enough theologian to recognize that trust in God is more important than claiming fully to understand God.

In a world in which both mystery and the desire to know are facts, doubt is inevitably a part of human experience. As children we believe many things implicitly on word of parent or teacher. This is the stage of raw credulity. As we grow older the facts of experience sometimes challenge what we have believed without question. Doubt enters the picture—and that can be painful indeed.

Yet, doubt has its work to do. To grow is to outgrow. To grow into more adequate ideas of God it is necessary to doubt and outgrow some less adequate concepts. Among life's growing pains there are the pains of honest doubting.

Alfred Tennyson once wrote

> There lives more faith in honest doubt,
> Believe me, than in half the creeds.

Some doubt can hardly be called honest doubt. It is more like cynicism or the will-to-disbelieve. On the other hand, honest doubt is an important reality. It is sometimes a part of the search for truth. One doubts, not because he enjoys doubting, but because he honestly believes his reason and the available evidence force him to question.

Doubt of this kind may actually reveal a kind of implicit faith. It reveals the desire to know the truth even though that may involve giving up some long-cherished ideas. Thomas Huxley once wrote a letter to Charles Kingsley in which he said, ". . . the longer I live the more obvious it is to me that the most sacred act of a man's life is to say and to feel 'I believe such and such to be true.' All the greatest rewards and all the heaviest penalties of existence cling about that act." Honest doubt sometimes reveals a dedication to the truth. And to seek the truth is to seek God.

Furthermore, the honest doubter believes that there is some sort of rational order or structure in the universe—otherwise reason would have no place. In his appeal to logic and to reason he is expressing a belief about the nature of things. And this is no small grain of faith! Yes, it is possible to experience God in the midst of the pain of doubt. Indeed, the living God sometimes prods and stirs us to seek greater understanding. We recall that Jesus called his followers to love God not only with heart, soul and strength—but with their minds. (Mark 12:30)

Let us turn now to a consideration of some of the feelings which attend depression. How painful they are! We all have our "down days and hours," our moods, our tides of the spirit. I once knew a person who condemned herself for feeling discouraged or "down" as she put it. "After all," she said, "a Christian ought to be above that sort of thing." Well, Christians are *not* above that sort of thing. Discouragement, fatigue of spirit, a measure of depression is a part of the lot of every human being.

To be sure, there are times when prolonged depression and persistent depth of depression, or extreme swings of feeling from deep depression to high elation, may indicate some underlying problem. The Christian should not hesitate to seek out professional help under these circumstances. It is no more a disgrace to seek help for our emotional problems than it is to seek it for our physical problems. Our bodies and spirits are wondrously interrelated. We sometimes need the special understandings of those who are trained in the interrelations of body and mind, matter and spirit. God sometimes works healingly through such persons.

At the same time, some swings of the emotional pendulum are to be expected. We ought not judge our spiritual health by the way we happen to feel at the moment. One ought not trust his feelings overly much in times of fatigue and loneliness. Feelings sometimes betray us. It is the direction of our willing and aspiring, the overall style of getting on which is more important.

We normally think of "devotional literature" as that which comes out of high tides of the spirit, when the sense of the presence of God is very real. But there are exceptions to this. If the Book of Psalms includes some of the greatest affirmations of faith ever written, it also includes plaintive cries coming out of darker moments. "Why dost thou stand afar off, O Lord? Why dost thou hide thyself in times of trouble?" (Psalm 10:1) "My God, my God, why hast thou forsaken me?'' (Psalm 22:1) "Why hast thou forgotten me? Why go I mourning because of the oppression of the enemy?'' (Psalm 42:9)

In the sixteenth century John of the Cross, a Spanish priest, wrote his famous work *The Dark Night of the Soul.* In this he speaks of that phase of the Christian life which might be called spiritual desolation, frustration, or even despair. It comes to those who having seen the vision of God, having known the presence of God, now feel that the vision has vanished and they are alone. John of the Cross acknowledges the pain of the dark nights of the soul. However, he believed that one ought not be inwardly defeated by these experiences—they may be a part of growing a little, of growing for awhile, and then withdrawing for awhile.

What can one do while passing through dark nights of the soul? There are several things: (1) One can recognize that such experiences are almost certainly going to be a part of our human experience. (2) One can go about one's usual duties, even though one's spirit may not be in it. (3) One can seek to get proper rest and food and exercise. (4) One can seek to do something for someone else. (5) One can mingle times of solitude with times of fellowship, especially with persons of mature faith. (6) One can pray and share in the worship of the community of faith. (7) One can seek to dedicate even his darker hours to the end that there might come some growth of spirit and some deeper understanding of the problems of those near at hand. (8) One can be open to God. "For God alone my soul waits in silence, for my hope is from him.'' (Psalm 62:5)

The experience of God is not confined to those hours when God seems near at hand and when our dominant feeling is that of joy and expectancy. God is also in our darker hours as one who sustains even in our weakness, as one who offers resources we sometimes know not of, as one who sometimes works redemptively through experiences which on the surface, seem all waste or evil.

Blessed is he who knowing doubt continues to seek understanding. Blessed is he who knowing depression, falls not into despair, but carries on waiting for light to break. No person walks alone. God is in our future, whatever that future may be.

Abraham Lincoln was a man of deep feeling. He experienced dark nights of the soul. He said that in such hours he was helped by recalling the words "even this will pass away." Who can doubt that knowing desolation of spirit, Lincoln came to feel more sympathetically with the hurts of others? Dr. Harry Emerson Fosdick has related his own experience of spiritual despair. It was out of the soil of that experience that he came to know the delivering, redeeming love of God in a new way. He has written: *"The Meaning of Prayer,* I think, would never have been written had not that year put into prayer a significance one does not learn from books." Thousands have been helped by Dr. Fosdick's book on prayer—a book which grew out of one man's dark night of the soul.

THE EXPERIENCE OF GOD—
IN HUMAN RELATIONSHIPS

Our greatest joys and our greatest sorrows so often come through human relationships.

When things are right in our human relationships there is a sense of well-being and of fulfillment. When things are wrong in our human relationships there is frustration, emptiness, and loneliness.

It is not strange that it should be so. By nature we are social creatures. We come into being, we are sustained, we are nurtured, we are spiritually formed *through relationships.* John Donne spoke truly when he said, "No man is an island unto himself." We are relational creatures. What life comes to mean to us depends in no small measure on what is happening in our human relationships.

The Sunday School Christmas program in a certain church was delayed because just as the participants were about to enter, a quarrel broke out among some of the eight-year-old angels! Yes, Christmas comes with its message of peace and goodwill, but it comes to a world in which we have great problems with our human relationships throughout life.

Can it be said that we experience God in the midst of our human relationships? Indeed we can. Jesus felt so strongly on this point that some of his most searching parables and statements have to do with human relationships. "So if you are offering your gift at the altar, and there remember that your brother has something against you, leave your gift there before the altar and go; first be reconciled to your brother, and then come and offer your gift." (Matthew 5:23-24) Love of God and man are inextricably interwoven, said Jesus. (Mark 12:28-31) The Sermon on the Mount (Matthew, chapters 5, 6, 7) is filled with references to human relations. Some of Jesus' most memorable parables, such as those of the Prodigal Son and the Good Samaritan, point to the connection between love of God and love of man. What, then, are some of the ways in which we experience God in the midst of our human relationships?

For one thing *we experience God in the provision that persons need each other*. God is the uniting, binding reality at the heart of life. That is why the profoundest human relationships always point beyond themselves. We need other persons, together with the work and influences of other persons, every day of our lives. But the richest human relationships are those in which persons share something more than their own company. They participate in that reality which underlies all life. Their relationship has a *transcendent dimension*. There is a sanctity in human relationships which reflects love of God and love of persons at the same time. The love of two persons goes deepest when they share a love of God.

We experience God through the built-in judgments which are a part of human relationships. There are some ways of relating which do not hold up; they seem to violate the very nature of reality: to treat other persons *as things*; to use persons only for one's own purposes; to exploit other persons without concern for their own welfare; to be unjust is to be judged and found wanting. Some styles of relating are self-defeating. God is present in the faithfulness and integrity which underlies life and which continually calls our lives into question.

We experience God in the grace which brings healing and forgiveness and wholeness through human relations. How painful it is to be estranged and alienated. How wonderful it is to experience forgiveness and reconciliation and new depth of relatedness. If God is present in those processes which bring judgment, he is also present in the coming of new depths of caring and belonging. God's love is experienced in those relationships which bring healing and fulfillment and wholeness.

We know that some relationships do not support, sustain, and enrich. Sometimes terrible things happen to persons through relations of antagonism, greed, exploitation, and insensitivity. God is in the pain of the judgment which comes with such relationships. Sometimes such relations seem to reach a point of no return. Sometimes it seems that the only road to integrity is through a realignment of relationships. Such decisions cannot be made easily. But God is present where there is integrity in decision-making, offering a love that undergirds and opens the door to new chapters of meaning. God does not plan or wish that every situation be as it is, but God is present in every situation seeking to bring something creative and redemptive out of it. Some of the dark nights of the soul are those in which human relations are being tried and tested and decisions are being made. God is present with us in those times, and a part of our worship of God is in the integrity and sensitivity with which we live through such testing chapters.

When all is said and done it is genuine love which justifies the struggles and pains of life. God's love is mediated through human love. And much of the love we offer God is given through love of his creatures. ". . . love is of God, and he who loves is born of God and knows God." (1 John 4:7)

God is present in the nurturing, healing, rehabilitating, educating work of persons, groups, and institutions which help persons to become what they have it in them to become. At the heart of the Christian gospel is the conviction that just as God has come to man in a human life, so God keeps coming to the world in human lives which bear witness to the living Christ. Where Christ's love is manifest, working its wonders of healing and growth and rehabilitation and new life we truly stand on holy ground.

How wondrous it is to see a parent or a teacher or a friend who understands what goes on in the hearts of persons, who knows that each chapter of life is meant for a particular kind of unfolding, and who "enables" persons to become more of what they have it in them to become. God uses human instrumentalities in his work of creation and recreation. How wonderful it is when we see groups and communities organizing in ways which will help to "set persons on their feet," and to surround persons with finer influences. God's continuing work of creation involves the creation of homes and schools and communities and institutions which help persons to relate more harmoniously and to live in more truly human ways. Participation in such creative efforts is part of our experience of God.

God is present in the living church—where persons relate to one another in worship, learning, reconciliation, serving, witnessing. The true church is not created out of sticks and stones and timber—not even out of committees and commissions, important as they are!

The living church is created out of *relationships*—informed by the living Spirit of Christ. "Where the spirit of the Lord is, there is the one true church, apostolic and universal."

In speaking of the church as the "body of Christ" Paul used the analogy of the physical body—various members relating in such a way that though there are many parts, there is one living body—a redemptive fellowship.

Tertullian, who lived from about 160 to 220, wrote of the Christians, "It is our care for the helpless, our practice of loving-kindness, that brands us in the eyes of many of our opponents. 'Only look,' they say. 'Look how they love one another. . . . Look how they are prepared to die for one another.' " Would that more of that spirit prevailed in many of our modern churches. But where it does, there the living Christ is present, there God's work of bringing new life is going on, there we truly experience God as we participate in his work of helping persons.

One who had gone through some devastating dark nights of the soul, who found strength to carry on through the church, came to know a new life in Christ. Speaking of her experience she said, "This church gave me back to myself." Where people are relating in caring, committed, Christian ways, new life is coming into being. God is being experienced there.

Throughout the world persons are hungry for true fellowship, true experience of community. We want and need to relate to each other *as persons*. In our feverish pursuit of material goals, in our emphasis on things and gadgets, we often miss the treasure of deep and creative human relationships. The church of Jesus Christ is called to show what deep community can really be. In commitment to Christ, in aspiration after the truly qualitative life, in caring for persons in their uniqueness, the living Christian fellowship comes into being. The persons close at hand and far away are those for whom Christ lived and died.

Such a fellowship cannot be brought into being through committees and commissions and planning alone. It comes into being out of the experience of God where persons in sincerity of purpose seek to probe the deeper levels of life's meaning, opening their lives to the Gracious Presence ever waiting to move in human hearts.

We experience God in building bridges of communication and understanding. We speak of the generation gap—and it can be real. But here are so many other gaps—between persons who are different—in race, nation, culture, creed. Increasingly it is clear that we are one family of man on "spaceship earth." Old ways of individualism and ruthless competition must give way to new ways of relating across barriers of language, culture, race. Where persons help to build bridges of communication and understanding and cooperation, there they participate in the presence and work of God.

It is given to each generation to move to some new frontiers of knowledge and experience. It is given our period of history to work at the task of creating one world in such a way that "we both keep the future safe and leave the future free." That is a part of what God is up to in our time. Each in his own time and place can have a part in that awesome and exciting work.

IN FACING UP TO THE MORAL CLAIMS OF LIFE

Charles R. Brown preached a famous sermon based on the parable of the Good Samaritan. He said that three philosophies of life are illustrated in the parable. There is the philosophy of the robbers: "What's yours is mine and I'll take it." There is the philosophy of the priest and Levite who passed by on the other side of the road: "What's mine is mine and I'll keep it." Finally, there is the philosophy of the Samaritan: "What's mine is ours and we'll share it." Here are the philosophies of selfish exploitation, of "respectable" indifference, and of human sharing.

We all have some philosophy of human relationships. We all have some theory as to what values we are looking for in and through these relationships. The study of ethics has to do with the *theory* of these matters. Morality is an *acting out* of our ethical theory. *Morality, in the deepest sense, is the search for values through our relationships with human beings and with our natural environment.*

When we speak of "moral values" we are speaking of values which hopefully can emerge out of relationships. All relationships are *potential for meaning*. A person's philosophy of life confronts an acid test in the question: "What values are you really seeking (or settling for) in your relationships?"

What are some of the relationships in which the moral question emerges? Our relationships with the good earth are so very important—we can exploit nature, we can try to be indifferent to it, or we can enter into creative, steward-like relations with it. There are relationships with individual persons on a one-to-one basis, in the family, in school, at work, in play, in various organizations, in church, in community. These relationships can be exploitive, they can reflect indifference, or they can bring forth enrichment of life for all concerned. There are relationships on levels where what we do influences other persons even though we do not meet personally. As citizens we share in making decisions on community, state, and national policy. What we do may have lasting influence on many persons. What values are we really concerned with creating and conserving through our institutions and political instrumentalities? This is a moral question. The seriousness with which we take our responsibilities as citizens is a moral issue.

There is a new urgency to the moral questions which Christians, along with all other human beings, must face in our time. With new powers over life and death man must now make decisions which only a few years ago we assumed were God's alone to make. Some of these decisions have to do with the stewardship of our natural environment. Some of them have to do with birth and death and the prolongation of life. Some of them have to do with the quality of education. Some of them have to do with the kind of future we hope for and the efforts we are willing to make on behalf of that future. *God has given man the power and responsibility for making awesome and wondrous decisions. And God is present with man in the making of those decisions when we bring depth of commitment to them.* It is a Christian conviction that persons are more than cogs in a machine and more than corks being buffeted about on a vast and indifferent sea. Man is bearer of the image of God—called to make decisions and thus to share in God's work of creation and recreation.

There are some Christians who sincerely believe that the experience of God is a purely individual matter, that God works in the inner life of persons. Some churchmen become unhappy when the church addresses itself to the world's larger moral issues. Some persons say, "The church ought to stick to preaching the gospel," meaning that the gospel has to do only with God's relations to individual persons. However, if we are going to take our place in that tradition which includes the Old Testament prophets, Jesus himself, the apostle Paul, the writers of the epistles, and such towering post-Biblical figures as Augustine, Thomas Aquinas, Francis of Assisi, Luther, Calvin and many contemporary Christians who have made their witness in relation to great issues of human relationships, we cannot in good faith rest content with a purely individual gospel. Christian morality has to do with the individual's values, aspirations and goals —but these have to do both with the inner life and with our varied human relationships. Wesley spoke of these matters with deep feeling: "Solitary religion is not to be found" in the gospel. "The Gospel of Christ knows no religion but social; no holiness, but social holiness." The world which God is continually seeking to create and to renew is not simply a physical world or universe. It includes the worlds of thought and feeling and relationship and spirit. Man is called to share in that creation.

Christian faith does not provide a set of rules or laws which give us simple answers to all complex questions. Obviously good laws are essential. Obviously we need guidelines in decision-making. But simple "this is what you must do now" rules are not available in many situations. Christians in the twentieth century are called to make decisions which were undreamed of in the first century.

What Christian faith does provide is an understanding of God and the love of God declared in Jesus Christ; an understanding of God's creating, renewing, humanizing presence in the world; an understanding of man both as sinner and bearer of the image of God—called to become ever more truly a center of freedom and of love; and an understanding of the world which God intends—a world (The Kingdom of God) in which God reigns in the hearts and relations of his creatures. The Christian is one who continually seeks to understand and to walk in the light of the gospel. He is one who seeks to make his decisions in the light of the understandings of God and man and destiny which are implicit in the gospel. In making his decisions the Christian inevitably will make some mistakes. Thus, he needs to seek continuing understanding and continuing forgiveness. Thus, he needs to seek continuing understanding and continuing forgiveness. He is not adequate to make his decisions alone, and so he needs the Christian fellowship which both calls to account and undergirds.

In the light of Christian understanding we come to see that morality is not just a private, subjective matter. In these days we are seeing much of privatism in the moral arena. "I want what I want when I want it." "Nothing is right or wrong in itself—thinking makes it so." "To be authentic one must be free to 'do his thing.' " "There are no objective guides in morals—it all comes from within." Statements such as these, and attitudes these statements reflect, are widespread. But Christian faith insists that life and relationships are not that simple. In life and death we are "up against" realities in nature, man, and God which we cannot escape. In the midst of our decision-making we are subject to what is deepest in reality. And in that Ultimate Reality we are both judged and offered grace and guidance.

Many of the situations in which we must make decisions offer no clear alternative between right and wrong. None of the alternatives before us offers a clear and satisfactory solution to a problem. Many of our decisions involve neither black nor white. They are in the "gray" area. Christian decision-making, like politics, is the "art of the possible." We must do the best we can do. There need be no self-condemnation because we have not come up with the ideal answer. But the fact that many situations are ambiguous does not mean that we are therefore excused from dealing with them. We must seek to do the best thing that can be done. God is present even in the relativities of life seeking to accomplish as much of good as can be accomplished.

On Christmas Day in 1968 a remarkable article appeared in the *New York Times*. One of America's Apollo missions was underway and the spacecraft was speeding around the moon. Astronauts were seeing planet Earth in a new way and from a new perspective. Under these circumstances Archibald McLeish wrote the article which appeared in the *Times*. He pointed out that there have been certain points in history when men have come to new knowledge and experience—and thus have been forced to break out of old perspectives and old ways of thinking into new perspectives and new life styles. Now, he said, we have come to such a time once more. A new kind of man, universal man, is needed. He wrote: "To see the earth as it truly is . . . is to see ourselves as riders on the earth together . . . brothers who know now that they are truly brothers." We are being given a new vision of a new world which calls for a new kind of person. God is calling us into a larger morality inspired by the vision of the whole person in a whole world.

In such an awesome period of history the church is called to play a larger part in helping persons in Christian decision-making. The church no longer can seek to avoid controversial issues. Life itself is controversial. The matters on which Christians must make decisions are often matters on which honest and sincere persons of goodwill can disagree. The church is not a fellowship of persons who think alike on all issues. Neither is it a fellowship which prizes consensus of thought so highly that it avoids all controversial issues. Rather, it is a fellowship of those honestly trying to live the Christian life, and honestly seeking answers which are faithful to the mind and spirit of Christ. Christians need each other to talk through these issues and to learn from one another. The Christian church is a communicating, caring, committed fellowship. Together the members of the body of Christ are seeking light on the question Dietrich Bonhoeffer expressed so well when he said, "It is becoming clearer every day that the most urgent problem besetting our Church is this: How can we live the Christian life in the modern world?"

In these matters it is important for the individual Christian to bear in mind that his personal influence is important. It is so easy to feel that one person is "just a drop in the bucket." But the moral strength generated by committed individuals working together becomes a mighty force in the history of the world. A single life can be attached to great causes and values. James Barrie spoke of persons who are "strong nails who hold the world together." In every community there are such persons—some of them in modest stations of life. Everyone of us can be a part of the answer to the world's need for caring and for strength. Everyone of us can make some contribution to the moral strength of our communities—and in that we truly enter into the life of God.

THE EXPERIENCE OF GOD—
IN SICKNESS AND IN HEALTH

We human beings are wondrous mixtures of body and spirit, matter and mind.

We do not simply live *in* our bodies, *we live our bodies*. Sometimes we talk about the spiritual life as though it were something quite independent of our bodily functions. Yet, increasingly we are learning that in the divine order body and spirit, mind and matter are deeply interrelated. If we are to speak of our experiences of God, we must reckon with God's presence in the pattern of creation which links these various aspects of our being. Human beings are born to be "whole" creatures—not just body, not just spirit.

The Old Testament affirms that "God created man in his own image . . . male and female he created them." (Genesis 1:27) "The earth is the Lord's and the fulness thereof, the world and they that dwell therein." (Psalm 24:1) Sometimes our bodies seem to get in the way of a deepening experience of God. Yet, there is much in our religious heritage as well as in contemporary experience which says it is unrealistic to talk about living a spiritual life without reference to living a bodily life. Somehow, they belong together. God's intention for human beings involves the experience of being *em-bodied*.

The body serves many purposes. We are *externalized* through our bodies. We *communicate* through our bodies. Much important communication takes place through the movements, postures, and expressions of our bodies. We share in *creation* by way of our bodies. We *learn* through our bodies. Through bodily senses we *perceive and experience the world in its qualitative richness.* In the order of divine creation *life, mind, and spirit emerge in relation to bodily processes.* The wisdom which underlies and inspires creation wondrously links the bodily and the spiritual, the material and the mental. Edmund Sinnott, the biologist, wrote, "My contention is not that we should stress the senses as against the spirit, but that the body, a necessary portion of our being, should contribute its rightful share not only to our enjoyment but to the development of the higher levels of Life." *(Matter, Mind and Man,* p. 80)

From personal experience and observation we know how physical states can influence mental states, and how attitudes and thoughts and mental factors can influence bodily states. Psychosomatic medicine is concerned with the relation of the physical and the psychological in the sickness and the health of human beings. Indeed, there is a connection between a person's self-esteem and the way he perceives and relates to his own body. To think of one's body as unworthy or unattractive is to be handicapped in one's own eyes and in one's relations to the world. To accept oneself as a person involves coming to a working relationship with the bodily dimension of one's being.

At the heart of things there is an organizing principle, a patternfulness, a purposiveness, a striving for goals. We discern it in protoplasm; we discern it in the processes of evolution, we discern it in human beings. Man is part of the natural processes, but in his capacity for reason, evaluation, appreciation, decision, and commitment the natural order comes to a new level of achievement. In the divine order life, mind, spirit are *achievements* in which natural, bodily experience has its role. Creative becoming is fundamental in the divine pattern. Our experience of God includes participation in the divine processes of *creative becoming*——and this includes committed, creative participation in the body-mind-spirit pattern of existence.

With this understanding we come to see that "soul" does not refer to a disembodied spirit. Rather, we use the term "soul" to refer to the wholeness God intends for man, a wholeness involving body, mind, spirit, sensitivity, love, inwardness linked with a caring relation to the world. There is a hunger for "soul" in today's world. But that hunger can never be satisfied by denying all that is bodily or natural. Rather, it must come by way of a deepening experience of God in the whole of life. The art of grace-ful living in this world involves finding the proper balances and relations between the parts which make the whole.

Against this background we see more deeply into the spiritual significance of sickness and of health. Most of us experience some of both; indeed, sickness and health are relative terms; often there is some of sickness and some of health in us at the same time. Sickness may be traced to a variety of things: imbalances in the organism, infection, injury——internally or externally imposed——deterioration. Some sickness is avoidable. Other sickness seems to involve factors beyond man's control. In the life of the spirit sickness has its place and its lessons to teach.

In the presence of any seeming adversity there are three prayers one can pray: for escape, for endurance, for the grace to elevate the experience into a living faith that something redemptive might come out of it. So it is with sickness. Through the healing processes we are delivered from some illnesses. There are resources, both physical and spiritual, to help us endure what must be endured. But is there anything more to be said? Many persons have shown us that there are important lessons to be learned and graces of spirit to be achieved through sickness.

Sickness reminds us of how dependent we are and how fragile life is. The gift of life is given us anew each minute, each hour, each day. But all of life is lived within limitations. We are finite creatures.

Sickness sometimes reminds us that there are "laws of health" to which we are subject. We cannot violate them without paying penalties. God is present in the same processes by which we fall ill and gain health—they are of a pattern.

Sickness is sometimes the occasion for being reminded of how kind and thoughtful and helpful people can be. There is a plaque on Denver General Hospital which reads:

Dedicated to the People of Denver As a Center For Health Care, So That They May Find Ready Help in Time of Need in an Atmosphere of Enlightenment and Kindness. . . . A Place Where Life Begins and Well-Being Is Fostered; Where Crisis Is Met and Life Is Celebrated.

Persons who serve us on a one-to-one basis, or persons who serve us as part of a hospital team often remind us in sickness of how much love and goodness there can be in the hearts of human beings.

In sickness we are reminded that there is within nature a will to resist illness and a will toward recovery. Our bodies share in this deep will, and healing sometimes comes as we work with it. God works toward wholeness. Healing is a wondrous fact involving much more than human planning, predicting, or producing.

In sickness we sometimes learn of God's presence and love in a new way. Louis Cassels, the syndicated columnist, suffered a heart attack. Later he wrote a column beginning with the sentence "Serious illness can be a blessing." He wrote, "I'm not trying to suggest that a hospital is a jolly place to be. It isn't." But then he went on to say that there is more to be taken into account. "The author of the 23rd Psalm glimpsed the basic reason, I think. When you walk through what is called 'the valley of the shadow of death' your natural fear can be quite remarkably allayed by a strong awareness that God is with you. . . . What He extends in an hour of real crisis is a sense of his presence—not magical protection from the natural consequence of your illness . . . in serious illness you can be aware of his presence and confident of his love to a degree not often attained in the peaceful and painless passages of everyday life."

More important still is the fact that through sickness persons sometimes achieve and exhibit great nobility of spirit. I had a sister who suffered from multiple sclerosis. She was bedridden for many years. Her life was a living witness to the truth of the words of scripture: "My flesh and my heart may fail, but God is the strength of my heart and my portion for ever." (Psalm 73:26) "So we do not lose heart. Though our outer nature is wasting away, our inner nature is being renewed every day." (2 Corinthians 4:16) From her life there radiated a faith and hope and love which strengthened and inspired many. My own life has been enriched more than I can say through her life. She once said that of course she would not choose this illness, but if these were the terms on which life was given her, she would not only make the most of it, she would seek to make something significant out of it, making her witness under these circumstances. Such lives demonstrate the victorious and resurgent power of Spirit.

What, then, shall we say of health? What a blessing it is! How grateful we should be for it. How sincerely we ought to guard it, honoring God in the care of the physical bodies we have been given. How important it is that we undergird those agencies and causes which seek to improve the health of individuals and communities.

But health is not only a matter of our physical bodies. There is also health of mind and spirit. These, too, need to be nurtured. Just as our bodies require wholesome food and proper diet, so our motions and our spirits need to be nourished through the ministries of beauty and of love.

Dr. Richard Cabot of the Harvard Medical School many years ago said that there are four things by which we truly live: work and play and love and worship. One of his students came to the time of retirement. He said, "Out of all of my years of practice I would give a prescription for health of the whole person. I would liken life to a table with four legs to be kept in balance: work and play and love and worship. Then, I would place a vase of flowers on the table to represent this very day—made more whole through the ministries of work and play and love and worship."

Yes, we may know God's presence and love—in sickness and in health.

"For everything there is a season . . . a time to be born, and a time to die." (Ecclesiastes 3:1-2)

Deep within we know that the words from the Book of Ecclesiastes are true. But in our hearts we resist their truth. We have difficulty accepting the fact of death. We are a death-denying, death-defying culture. Death so often seems to be the great intruder into life. So, we talk about our philosophies of *life;* less often do we talk about our philosophies of *death.* We celebrate *life;* but how strange it seems to speak of celebrating *death.*

There are, tragically, untimely deaths. We think of deaths caused by accident, war and other violence. We think of the deaths of persons young in years with so much of possibility for creative living in them. Such deaths force us to search our faith as we ponder the fact that our world involves the possibility of such untimely losses. Each day of life involves risk. Yet, we know that in the divine order life and death are interrelated. Life feeds into death and death feeds into life. My life is possible because others before me have died. My death will help to make possible the life of another. The world space is limited. We never really come to terms with life until we have come to some philosophy or theology of death. Dag Hammarskjold said, "In the last analysis, it is our conception of death which decides our answers to all the questions that life puts to us."

Profound religion faces the fact of death. "Thou turn-

est man back to the dust. . . . The years of our life
are threescore and ten." (Psalm 90:3, 10) But profound religion does not stop with a stoic resignation
to what must be. In the conviction that God is with
us, both in our living and in our dying, great faith
goes on to affirm the life-death cycle in trust, in hope,
in expectation. In this spirit Francis of Assisi com-
posed his beautiful *Canticle of Brother Sun* including
the words:

Praised be Thou, my Lord, for Brother Wind,
For air, for weather cloudy and serene,
    and every weather
By which Thou to Thy creatures givest sustenance.

. . . .

Praised be Thou, my Lord, for our brother bodily
    Death
From whom no living man can ever escape.

If God is truly present in the deep, mysterious and
wondrous patterns linking life and death, God is also
present in the provision for grief which is the price of
love. Grief is not to be denied. The shock and pain
involved in the death of one who is near and dear
shakes our whole being. Our whole self *protests*.
We are likely to experience *despair*. There may be
times of *detachment* marked by psychological isola-
tion, apathy and hopelessness. Instead of denying
these facts of experience we need to *live through
them*. Only so can we come to be open to the healing
resources of friendship and of faith. Only so can we
move into the experience of *reorganization* with the
feeling that one wants to go on living, and one feels
more free to take the risks of reaching out to life
again. A part of our experience of God is in the experience of these painful but healing chapters of life.

He who has never grieved has never loved in depth. But he who loves is more free to grieve—and then to go beyond grief. Grief has its work to do.

In speaking of persons who had found Christ through the early Methodist societies John Wesley said, "Our people die well." The fact of the matter is that all of us, from the beginning of life, are in the process of dying. Living and dying are that intimately related. To die well (in the awareness that every day we are moving toward death) means to turn the dying processes to spiritual ends. How can this be?

For one thing, *the life-long process of dying can contribute to the birth of a new self and new selves.* The awareness that life has time-limits—that *my* life comes to an end in this earthly pilgrimage—forces one to make decisions. It forces us to set priorities; to determine what values we propose to put first; to decide in what we are going to invest our time, talent, energies. In these decisions we decide who and what we propose to be. As the years pass life increasingly tends to be a matter of dissipation or dedication. Our acts of dedication and commitment are acts of choosing what self we will be. Thus, dying makes its contribution to God's creative work in and through ourselves.

> Die and Become.
> Till thou hast learned this
> Thou art but a dull guest
> On this dark planet.
> (Goethe, 1749-1832)

The awareness that we are moving toward death may deepen our awareness of the preciousness of each day. Life is too short to be little. Having recovered, in some measure, from an illness which might well have terminated his life, Abraham Maslow spoke of the wonder of being given a "postmortem life." He said: ". . . everything gets doubly precious. . . . You get stabbed by things, by flowers and by babies and by beautiful things—just the very act of living, of walking and breathing and eating and having friends and chatting. Everything seems to look more beautiful rather than less, and one gets the much-intensified sense of miracles.

The awareness that we are moving toward death may deepen our awareness that life has basic patterns to which we can relate. The seasons of life: infancy, childhood, youth, young adulthood, the middle years, the later years somehow fit together. There are certain achievements or "developmental tasks" appropriate to each. Life is intended to have a cumulative dimension. Something coming out of each chapter of life which enriches and strengthens the next chapters. It is part of the divine intention that we "go from strength to strength." (Psalm 84:7) Thus, moving toward death in the midst of life confronts each of us with the questions: What is the harvest of your years of living? To what is it adding up? Is your life flattening out or flowering out? How tragic if we have nothing but years to prove our age! How wonderful it is when with the passing years the inner light shines more brightly and one's hoping and loving become more real. "So teach us to number our days that we may get a heart of wisdom." (Psalm 90:12)

The awareness that we are moving toward death may deepen our relationship with God. It does not always work out that way, but sometimes it does. Some people are embittered by the awareness that death comes to all. Some attempt to deny or evade the fact. Some try to resign themselves to the fact—but without meaning. Still others have learned that one can dedicate every basic experience, including that of dying. In that spirit Pierre Teilhard de Chardin prayed, ". . . *teach me to make a communion of death itself.*" In his last hours John Wesley endeavored to sing the hymn which meant so much to him:

> I'll praise my Maker while I've breath;
> And when my voice is lost in death,
> Praise shall employ my nobler powers.
> My days of praise shall ne'er be past,
> While life, and thought, and being last,
> Or immortality endures.

There are those who show us that one may live and die to the glory of God.

The discovery that in the divine order life and death are so intimately related may lead to a deepening understanding of eternal life. It is not given man to know much that he would like to know. Living with mystery is part of human finitude. So there is much about the future we cannot know. But it *is* given the Christian to be assured that "neither death, nor life . . . nor any thing else in all creation, will be able to separate us from the love of God in Christ Jesus our Lord." (Romans 8:38-39) "None of us lives to himself, and none of us dies to himself. If we live, we live to the Lord, and if we die, we die to the Lord; so then, whether we live or whether we die, we are the Lord's. (Romans 14:7-8) Augustine wrote, "Blessed be he who loves thee, and his friend in thee, and his enemy for thee. For he alone loses no one dear to him to whom all are dear in thee who never can be lost."

In his book *And The Life Everlasting* John Baillie tells of the Scotch physician who was attending a close personal friend in his last hours. The friend asked,

"Tell me, you are a believer of sorts. What will it be like—after I die?" There was a moment of silence. Suddenly there was a scratching at the bedroom door. The doctor turned to his friend and said, "Did you hear that? It's my dog. He's been waiting for me downstairs and has become impatient. He has never been in this room. He has no idea what it is like. He knows only one thing about it and that is that *I'm here*. . . . That's all I know about the future. . . . He's there." In a similar vein E. Stanley Jones said on his eightieth birthday, "I don't know what the future holds, but I do know who holds the future." God is in life and in death and nothing shall separate us from the love of God.

With this understanding *eternal life* takes on depth of meaning. It is a life which cannot adequately be measured by clocks and calendars. The Gospel of John cites the prayer, "And this is eternal life, that they know thee the only true God, and Jesus Christ whom thou hast sent." (John 17:3) Eternal life is defined not by length of days or years, but by depth of relationship to God. That life can be real in our todays and in our tomorrows. We experience many little deaths along the way. In those very deaths our experience of eternal life can begin and be renewed and be deepened. Eternal life begins when our relationship with God is so real and meaningful that in the midst of time we have an inner relationship which overcomes the tyranny of time. Samuel Miller wrote, "Eternity is mixed with the stuff of this earth. Eternity begins whenever and wherever we are able to transcend the present dimensions of our living and become greater and greater souls." *(The Life of the Soul.)*

It has been said that some people yearn for endless

life who don't know what to do with a rainy afternoon. The blessedness of a deep and abiding relationship with God cannot be measured simply in temporal terms. That is why we use the term *eternal* life. There can be something of the eternal even in rainy afternoons—even as there is in all the mornings, afternoons, evenings, and dark nights which God gives to man. "From everlasting to everlasting thou art God." (Psalm 90:2b)

The awareness that we all share in the divine pattern of living and dying may kindle a deepened sensitivity to those about us. We differ in many ways, but we are all given the gift of life and we all are moving toward death. Beneath the surface of their lives all the people around us are living in the knowledge that the days of life are numbered.

How important it is that we mean something to each other in our living and in our rejoicing and in our grieving and in our dying. The Christian church is a fellowship of the caring; Christian caring encompasses the whole range of human experience. How tragic that we should ever neglect persons when perhaps they need us most.

A number of books have been published in recent years dealing with death and dying. Such studies as have been made indicate that grieving and dying persons need to be understood and cared about and communicated with in the depths of their hurting and their fearing. In many instances hearing is the sense a person maintains longest in his closing hours. Sometimes the spoken word communicates more than we know. But there is also communication in the touch of the hand and sometimes in shared silence. The gospel tells us of the divine love which is *always there.* As Christians we are called to be human instruments of that love.

We often hesitate or fear to think of death—our own or that of those dearest to us. It is natural that it be so. But to our deepest fears and anxieties and questions comes the assurance of the gospel. The deepest word to man is not a word of condemnation or despair, but the word of grace and hope. In the faith of the gospel we may pray for the grace to make a communion of death itself. We may offer the prayer which has meant so much to so many:

O Lord, support us all the day long of this troublous life, until the shadows lengthen, and the evening comes, and the busy world is hushed, and the fever of life is over, and our work is done. Then in thy mercy grant us a safe lodging, and a holy rest, and peace at the last; through Jesus Christ our Lord. Amen.

THE EXPERIENCE OF GOD—
WHEN THE GOSPEL IS REALLY HEARD

Several recurring themes run through the chapters of this book:

1. Our deepest and most enduring relationship is with God.

2. The Christian understanding of God is grounded in the living experience of God. God is known experientially in the world of nature which testifies to the order, dependability, and creative power of God. God is known experientially in the accepting, forgiving, healing, renewing love declared and mediated in Jesus Christ. God is known experientially in the energizing presence of the Holy Spirit—enabling, instructing, kindling faith, inspiring, leading into newness of understanding, summoning into service and witness. In seeking a deepening understanding and experience of God the Christian turns to the resources of scripture, tradition, experience, and reason.

3. The experience of God is not confined to one event or to one segment of life. There are high moments of discovery and illumination and transformation for many. But God acts somewhat differently in every life. God is experienced not only at particular points, but also in the continuities and relationships of life and in the basic processes of life and growth and death. As John Calvin said, "A Christian man ought to be so disposed and prepared as to reflect that he has to do with God every moment of his life."

4. In Christian perspective, life is intended to be

more than a series of events and experiences, pleasant and unpleasant. There is pattern and purpose running through the order of creation. The human creature has a distinctive place in the divine scheme. Man is born to be reborn; he born for creative becoming; he is born to move through the stages of utter self-centeredness and immature rebelliousness toward becoming a center of freedom and of love. The high destiny to which the human creature is called involves for more than being a cog in a machine, a rat in a rat race, a consumer in a vast production system. He is born to move toward wholeness in a whole world, ". . . to mature manhood, to the measure of the stature of the fullness of Christ; . . . speaking the truth in love, we are to grow up in every way into him who is the head, into Christ." (Ephesians 4:13-15)

5. The gospel is the supreme good news to persons in their actual situations. It brings the word of grace and hope and possibility. To persons bogged down in apathy, smugness or boredom, to persons bowed down with guilt or grief, to persons hungering for a meaning in life they have not found, the gospel says, "Lift up your hearts. Hear the good news. It is good news for *you*."

But here we come to a crucial point. Many persons hear the *words* of gospel—but they do not hear the gospel as being *good news for them*.

Is it not amazing how persons can hear the gospel—spoken and written in words, portrayed in art, sung out in music, enacted in great ritual, and still go unmoved—responding oftentimes with a yawn? Probably in Jesus' time many persons saw him and heard him but passed on unmoved. They did not hear his message as being a message *for them. The experience of God is real in the hearing of the gospel as good news addressed to oneself.*

When, then, is the gospel really heard as being good news for oneself? To that important question there is one basic answer. *The gospel is really heard when it comes as a response to the deepest and most ultimate questions we ask. The gospel becomes good news for oneself at the point that one decides to commit and order his life in the light of the gospel.* At the point of commitment gospel becomes more than theory. It becomes one's basic grip on life and on reality.

Drawing on the experience of many persons whose lives have been changed and renewed through the gospel we can make several statements. They have to do with what happens in one's inner life when the gospel comes through as *good news for oneself.* Although these precise words may not be used, something like the following thoughts and feelings are expressed:

I see life in a new way. Its real meaning is more clear.
My life style is called into question. My values need straightening out.
New possibilities are opened before me.
I am not alone. God is with me and for me.
I am summoned into a new life of commitment, trust, service, and witness.
There is a joy and peace I have never known before.
The gospel is for all persons. God wills whole persons in a whole world.

The gospel of God's creating, renewing presence puts everything in a different light. Life is seen as having purpose. One's own life is precious and has importance. There is a sanctity in all existence—persons and things and relationships.

The gospel makes us see how thin and gasping and

pointless so much of our existence sometimes is. We put our trust in the idols of power, position, possessions. We miss the higher blessedness for which we are born. Thus, we are judged in the light of the gospel. Our values need reordering.

The gospel opens new possibilities. Life can have a joy and meaningfulness and depth we often miss. Life is pilgrimage—pilgrimage into a growing life of faith and hope and love. Each day can have the touch of the eternal upon it, as our daily duties, relationships, activities are dedicated to the higher ends of life. God can be experienced in each today. The gospel shows how each and every day we live "by grace." Life is a gift. We are sustained and nurtured by the god in whom "we live and move and have our being." There is a love which makes life worth the living, bringing healing and wholeness. In the personal experience of God there is a peace and joy which comes no other way.

The gospel brings a summons to commitment, trust, service, witness. The gospel reminds us that no person can live to himself alone. We are linked with all creation—human and nonhuman, organic and inorganic. We are called to place our personal stamp of trusting and hoping and loving on the world. We are called to share in God's work of creating a world which is "habitable"— good for growth of body, mind, and spirit. Christian commitment involves a profound inner dedication of one's own life. But that commitment does not stop with concern for self. It issues in new relationships. It issues in responsible citizenship.

In all these ways the gospel points up the difference between being barely human and being fully human, between bare existence and real life. We make a choice. Our daily choices and commitments reveal whether the gospel has become one's own.

There is a life worth living. Struggle is in it. Pain is in it. Loss is in it. Difficult decisions are in it. But growth is also in it. Victories of the spirit are in it. Sensitivity to goodness and beauty and truth are in it. A growing concern for persons is in it. A new kind of self-acceptance and self-respect is in it. Love of God and neighbor is in it. *And joy is in it.* "Thanks be to God for his inexpressible gift!" (2 Corinthians 9:15)

Every generation of Christians tries to put into words the wonder of new life in Christ. No matter what words are used they miss the full reality of the wonder of God's working in the minds and hearts and relationships of human beings. But we must keep trying to say what can never be fully expressed. How can one adequately speak of the experience of forgiveness, of new inner assurance, of a turning Godward in trust and commitment, of a deliverance from some of the motives and weights which have shackled our spirits, of a growth in love which reaches farther and deeper in relation to the world, to other human being, to God?

For these profound experiential realities such words as these have been used: justification, the witness of the spirit, conversion, sanctification, growth in grace, perfection. These are time-honored words. But the words point to what is deeper—God's gracious working in the souls and relationships of persons. The love of God, so wondrously declared in Jesus Christ, does bring new life. It is a life which seeks the actualization of God's rule in the human community—the kingdom of God. It is the new life of which the gospel speaks. It is a life for which we can decide. In that decision the gospel is both heard and received as one's own.

Out of personal experience Paul wrote, "I am not ashamed of the gospel: it is the power of God for salvation to every one who has faith, to the Jew first and also to the Greek. For in it the righteousness of God is revealed through faith for faith; as it is written, 'He who through faith is righteous shall live.'" (Romans 1:16-17)

These words came to have a kindling meaning to Martin Luther as he was searching for a deeper personal experience of God. John T. McNeill, distinguished church historian, calls the roll of persons who have heard the gospel as good news *for them*. He writes, "Whether suddenly or slowly, they were inwardly born anew, and filled with gratitude for a redemptive power that laid hold on them." He concludes, "The Gospel *is* good news, and there is no other tidings so momentous that we can hear or speak."

(*The Protestant Credo,* pp. 102, 124)

EPILOGUE

CHRISTIAN COMMITMENT— IN A WORLD COMING TO BE

A new world is coming into being. The world refuses to stand still. We cannot return to the past. What, then, does the future hold?

We are being told that the future of the human race on Planet Earth is a question. Mankind's continuation is threatened by pollution of air and soil and water, by overpopulation and poverty, by war. It is not only man's *physical* existence which is in question. In a society which is increasingly mechanized there is the danger that the human creature will become less human, that he will be transformed into the likeness of the machine—mechanical, unalive, devoid of great visions or deep feeling. With these things in mind Nicolas Berdyaev asked the question ". . . is that being to whom the future belongs to be called man . . . or something other?"

In such a time and in such a situation we can deny or evade the facts. We can retreat into individualism and subjectivism. We can resign ourselves to "whatever happens." Or we can ask, "Where is hope and how can I participate in that hope?" The Christian says that our ultimate hope is in God—but the hope which is of God must be mediated through persons, groups, families, communities and institutions which place the stamp of hoping on the world. The ancient biblical account says that God came to be profoundly disappointed in his human creature. "And the Lord was sorry that he had made man on the earth, and it grieved him to his heart." (Genesis 6:6) But the story does not end there. The biblical drama unfolds telling how God's grace is mediated to the world through the remnant, the suffering servant, the dying and loving and living Christ, the community of faith which becomes the Body of Christ in the world. Yes, there is hope, but a hope "become flesh" in committed, caring persons and groups. The word must become flesh again and again in the midst of the agony and the ecstasy of human existence.

A clearer vision is being given us in our time. The universe is vaster than we had ever dreamed. Planet earth is part of a cosmic spectacular we are just beginning to explore. We do not know what forms of life may exist on other heavenly bodies, but we are told that the conditions for life probably exist on multitudes of heavenly bodies. It is being given us to know that on Spaceship Earth there is a human race—born to be a family of man. We are part of a *cosmic whole* and a *human whole* from which we cannot resign. A living hope involves coming to a greater vision than we have ever had before. *The vision of whole persons in a whole universe.*

Such a vision reminds us that relationships are of fundamental importance in our continuing existence: relationships with the natural world about us, relationships with individual persons, relationships with groups and institutions, relationships in communities, relationships with governments, relationships with other races and cultures and nations, relationships with their ULTIMATE REALITY MAKING FOR WHOLENESS—GOD.

It is now being given us to see dimensions of the Christian gospel we have often missed. The God of Christian faith is a God of relationships. We experience God in the establishing of relationships which support, enhance and nurture life and human well-being. We experience God as we participate in efforts to overcome the fragmentation and the estrangements of the world—bringing more of understanding, communication, caring, cooperation, creative interchange.

The God who makes "all things new" is now calling for a new kind of person in a new kind of world. This person is one inspired by a growing vision of God's presence and purposes in the world. He is a person who is reordering his priorities and values in the light of the growing vision. He is a sensitive person. He is a person excited by the prospect and privilege of participating creatively in the coming of a new kind of world—a world good for the growth of persons becoming centers of freedom and of love. Thus, the wonder of the Christian gospel reaches into the depths of man's personal life offering a redemptive power and love which transforms life. It also reaches into our human relationships interpersonal, community-wide and world-wide.

There are three basic kinds of commitment which the Christian can now make. These commitments are of crucial importance if faith is to be translated into the fundamental relationships of life in the twentieth century. Through these commitments we express our readiness to become a part of the remnant which brings faith and love to the world of now. Through these commitments we help tip the scales between apathy and despair and fatalism on the one hand, and creative hope on the other.

First, there are the commitments which attend what we propose to do with our lives. They have to do with our personal relationship to God and Christ. They have to do with what we want to be central in our trusting and serving. They have to do with our own centers of value and centers of aspiring. Who do I propose to be and *whose* do I propose to be? Commitments on this level are of crucial importance. Not until we have faced up to them are we really prepared to go on to the others.

Second, there are the commitments which attend our involvement in the basic institutions of society which so profoundly influence the direction of human becoming: the family, the educational institutions, the state, community agencies, communication media. Day after day, hour after hour these institutions and agencies are molding human lives. Are we releasing influences which lead persons to fear and hate and conform? Or are we releasing influences which nurture persons who can trust and love and experiment and create? The answer is crucial for whatever future mankind is to have. Christian commitment on our time involves commitments in the area of responsible citizenship.

Third, there are the commitments we make in relationship to the community of faith—the Church. Are we looking for a church which simply reflects what we want to believe and feel and do? Or are we open to *being* a church which is truly Christ's and which seeks to follow his lead into the many relationships of today's world? How desperately our society needs a church which can communicate a great vision of reality, of human destiny, of the significant life in its worship, in its preaching and teaching, in its ministries of service and witness. How desperately the world needs a church whose members give witness to the fact that there is a new life in Christ, that there is a love which reaches out to all sorts and conditions of men, that there is a will to build bridges of communication and caring across barriers of race and nation and creed.

This book began with the suggestion that we must begin where we are. We need the courage to go beyond where we are. It has spoken of the wonder and the hope of the Christian gospel. It closes on the note of commitment. The God who creates us with the possibility of becoming centers of freedom and of love does not coerce in the deep things of the spirit. His power and love is manifest in the capacity for choice which is ours.